# Shamanic Healing for Toxic Relationships

"This splendid book is a crystal-clear guide to shamanic healing of ourselves and our relationships. I'm glad that *Shamanic Healing for Toxic Relationships* is now available in English. I wholeheartedly recommend it to anyone who wants to be a self-empowered and happier human being."

—**CARLOS PHILIP GLOVER**, shamanic coach
and author of *Earth Wisdom Teachings*

"What a gift this book is. I marvelled at its clarity and the author's successful endeavour to present and weave together key elements of maps through (amongst other terrains) psychology and shamanism. The complexity of being human and finding ourselves welded into invisible and heavy patterns is faced head on. Kindness, encouragement, and strength is the tone of mentorship all the way through. The author brings us what so many caught in these webs are needing: a compassionate manual that provides tools for release and means for spiritual and neurological reawakening. Stepping out of this book is like emerging into a new world theatre where you realize even more truly that your life is your own, ready to be taken by the horns, and that everything that has ever happened has been an invitation to explore and unlock even deeper freedom and meaning."

—**CAROL DAY**, psychotherapist, artist, and
author of *Shamanic Dreaming*

# SHAMANIC HEALING FOR TOXIC RELATIONSHIPS

### DISSOLVE OLD SOUL CONTRACTS AND RETRIEVE LOST SOUL PARTS

## STEFAN LIMMER

Translated by Hilary Snellgrove

**FINDHORN PRESS**

Findhorn Press
One Park Street
Rochester, Vermont 05767
www.findhornpress.com

Findhorn Press is a division of Inner Traditions International

---

### Disclaimer

The information in this book is given in good faith and is neither intended to diagnose
any physical or mental condition nor to serve as a substitute for informed medical
advice or care. Please contact your health professional for medical advice and treatment.
Neither author nor publisher can be held liable by any person for any loss or damage
whatsoever which may arise from the use of this book or any of the information therein.

---

Cataloging-in-Publication data for this title is available from the Library of Congress

ISBN 979-8-88850-249-5 (print)
ISBN 979-8-88850-250-1 (ebook)

Printed and bound in the United States by Lake Book Manufacturing, LLC

10 9 8 7 6 5 4 3 2 1

Edited by Nicky Leach
Illustrations by Nadia Gasmi (p. 133); Shutterstock (p. 135); Syndication: seasons.agency
Text design and layout by Richard Crookes
This book was typeset in Adobe Garamond Pro

To send correspondence to the author of this book, mail a first-class letter to the author
c/o Inner Traditions • Bear & Company, One Park Street, Rochester, VT 05767, USA
and we will forward the communication, or contact the author directly at
**https://schamanenpfad.de.**

# CONTENTS

## 1

## Toxic Relationships

## 2

## Soul Issues and Soul Wounds –
## The Real Causes of Toxic Relationships

# 3

## Ways Out of Toxic Relationship Patterns and Toxic Relationships

# PREFACE

We would all like relationships that enrich us, in which we are acknowledged and respected, have no need to pretend, and are accepted for who we are. In good relationships, this forms the basis for our life together. In toxic relationships, we have a completely different situation. Due to the toxic personality structure of one or more of those involved, these relationships are poisoned, often resulting in the suffering of everyone involved – and life together becomes torture. Those concerned often find no way out and are left feeling powerless, trapped, and dependent. If we want to permanently free ourselves from a toxic relationship and prevent ourselves from slipping back into similar patterns in the future, we need to track down the causes at the soul level, look at the underlying issues and patterns, and heal them. In this way, we create the conditions for fulfilling, happy relationships in which everyone involved respects, honours, and appreciates everyone else.

I myself grew up in an environment characterized by various toxic relationship structures, with all the negative consequences. My parents' relationship, in particular, was a prime example of what we now call a toxic relationship. They made life hell for themselves and those in their immediate environment.

I had to work on myself for a long time to recognize the patterns that had shaped me and that I had partly internalized, and to heal my own behaviour. This enabled me to have fulfilling relationships that nourish me and my environment and allow me to grow—relationships in which I can show who I am, instead of conforming, hiding, belittling myself, and falling back on the behaviours I internalized in my childhood.

It took me a long time to understand why my parents didn't separate and end this ordeal. Objectively speaking, such relationships are irrational, with both partners locked in a spiral of emotional abuse, verbal violence, and humiliation, culminating in physical violence; yet no one dares leave, a phenomenon that is difficult to understand. Today, I know that mutual dependency and entanglement keep those involved stuck in these patterns, and how difficult it is to break free from them if the soul has not been healed.

I explored many different psychological approaches on my path to self-healing and finding my way out of this dilemma, until finally I came across shamanism. In shamanism, I found ways to track down and heal the wounds that were deeply rooted in my soul. At the same time, I was able to recognize the underlying causes that lead us to persist in toxic behaviours and structures and not embark on the path to liberation and healing.

I have had personal experience with all the methods and paths I present in this book and have later accompanied clients in applying them. I have also developed or adapted many methods myself. The result is a shamanic soul path that reveals profound solutions, showing us how we can free ourselves from the prison of toxic relationship patterns in order to live permanently happy, nourishing, and fulfilling relationships.

I wish you an insightful journey that enables you to find a way out of your toxic relationships.

**Stefan Limmer**,
Regensburg, April 2021

**1**

# TOXIC RELATIONSHIPS

You and I – we are one.
I cannot hurt you without hurting myself.

~ *Mahatma Gandhi (1869–1948)*

# REALITY AND ILLUSION

So far, the term "toxic relationship" has mainly been used for partnerships. This is certainly where we find its strongest manifestations and where the toxic elements are often very clearly visible, due to the fact that we associate certain ideas of love, security, acceptance, and happiness with a love relationship. If these expectations are not met, we are often greatly disappointed and quick to judge certain elements and behaviours characteristic of our partner negatively.

However, this book is not only about toxic love relationships; it is also about toxic friendships and acquaintances, toxic family systems, toxic work relationships, and toxic company structures.

But what is a toxic relationship? Since many relationships contain elements and behaviours that we define as being toxic, it is difficult to give a clear definition. The transitions from a normal relationship to a toxic one are often fluid. This is less about a clear, rational perspective and more about individual perception. How are your relationships going? How do you feel when you are together or working with other people? Which feelings prevail?

> Romantic relationships are not the only ones that can be toxic. Friends, work colleagues, or members of your family can also display toxic behaviour.

## Looking Reality in the Eye

In discussions with clients and sufferers, I have seen repeatedly that it often takes a long time for people to lay aside their illusions, their hopes, and their tendency to sugar-coat everything and look reality in the eye. This is certainly due to the fact that relationships that later turn out to be toxic seem more like Heaven on Earth at the beginning. We believe we have finally found our dream partner. We have finally landed in a company where we have only nice colleagues and a wonderful boss. We finally feel understood by our new friends and have a great deal of fun together. That is why we invest so much time and energy. We put our heart and soul into the relationship, relax, allow ourselves to be lulled into a sense of security, open up, and reveal a great deal about ourselves.

When, after a while, our initial euphoria turns out to be an illusion and subsequently, in most cases, gradually gives way to bitter reality, when it becomes apparent that the person—or people—in whom we have placed so much hope are increasingly degrading, hurting, manipulating, and using us, then it is difficult to accept this truth.

We prefer to cling to our memories of beautiful beginnings.

We believe and hope that everything will go back to how it was at the beginning, when we were floating on Cloud Nine. We talk ourselves out of reality and suppress the obvious fact that the relationship is nourishing us less and less and is instead costing us more and more energy and destroying our feeling of self-worth. We don't want to recognize the power games, emotional blackmail, and manipulation that are increasingly affecting us and our well-being. We don't want to admit to ourselves that the energy of the relationship is acting like a poison on us and is slowly but surely making us ill. We hope that everything will go back to how it was in the beginning.

So we invest even more energy, put up with all the humiliating behaviour, allow ourselves to be debased and belittled, always hoping that we are only imagining things and that the other person will change for the better again and that everything will go back to how it was in the beginning. This exacerbates the downward spiral even more. We belittle ourselves, become even more vulnerable, and slide deeper and deeper into the toxic relationship. We forget our sovereignty and our own strength. We sacrifice ourselves and increasingly allow ourselves to become a plaything for the sensitivities and the sick, inhumane behaviour of our partner, boss, friend, mother, father, and others.

For people who have never experienced a toxic relationship, it may be incomprehensible as to why someone would allow themselves to be treated in this way and even defend those who degrade and manipulate them; why the people in question set no clear boundaries, if they are not being respected, and free themselves from these relationships. Even those concerned often don't understand why they cannot let go and choose to remain in an obviously unbearable relationship.

This is caused by certain elements and patterns within the psyche that are always similar or even identical and prevent us from simply freeing ourselves and ending the relationships concerned. This has become apparent in my work with clients and sufferers, as well as in my own experiences with toxic relationships.

Let us first look at how we can recognize a toxic relationship.

# INDICATORS OF TOXIC RELATIONSHIPS

How can we determine whether our relationships contain toxic elements? One key is that those involved take on certain roles—victim, perpetrator, and rescuer (see pages 22–31)—and this role model forms the basis of the relationship. However, it is not uncommon for those involved to swap roles. The following statements describe the situation from the victim's perspective, but you may also recognize yourself in the role of the perpetrator:

○ You frequently feel uncomfortable. You are often not able to understand exactly why that should be so, but you realize that something is wrong.

○ You feel as if you are being taken advantage of. Somehow you end up with all the work. Your toxic opposite keeps managing to delegate work to you, even though it is actually (also) theirs. You are becoming the general dogsbody to an ever greater degree and have less and less time for your own interests.

○ You feel small and inferior and are never good enough. No matter how hard you try, you are constantly criticized and your achievements are not appreciated. You gradually lose your feeling for whether you are doing something right or wrong. There is nothing you can rely on.

Your toxic opposite number:

o Your opposite number has permanent mood swings. You never know where you stand. One minute they are in a good mood, the next they are aggressive, angry, dismissive, and so on, and blame their moods on you. Even if there is no reason for it and you have no idea what you have done wrong yet again, you are made to understand that it is all your fault.

o One minute you are the centre of attention, the next you are being completely ignored. One minute your opposite number is showing you love and complimenting you, the next they are depriving you of their love and insulting you, ignoring you, and punishing you with indifference.

o Your opposite number is deliberately manipulating you with their whims and mood swings, blaming and hurting you, and so on. You do what they want you to do in the hope that you will win their attention, recognition, or affection.

o Your opposite number is rarely balanced and instead fluctuates between extremes.

o You no longer dare to be open about how you are feeling.

o You are pretending and playing a role that doesn't correspond to your true nature.

o Everything you do or say leads to misunderstandings and is misinterpreted. No matter what you say, it will always be twisted and used against you.

o You are neglecting other friendships and contacts. Your toxic opposite number manipulates you here too and puts down your friends, family, colleagues, and others. They criticize your hobbies and your interactions with other people, zeroing in on others' weaknesses as unacceptable behaviour and prohibiting you from further contact and interactions.

o Discussions are not constructive and almost always end in an argument, which is, of course, your fault.

o Your opposite number exploits your every weakness, no matter how small, and hurts you and instils feelings of guilt in you.

o Although you are the one being used and manipulated, you still find a reason to defend your opposite number and explain to yourself or others why everything is really not so bad.

o Your energy dwindles, and you are completely exhausted. To stop being exposed to this constant stress, you agree with everything your opposite says and deny your own self. You feel powerless and no longer have any connection to yourself, your self-love and self-worth, or your inner strength and vigour.

If we take the actions of our toxic opposite number as our starting point, we can identify the following characteristics and behaviours in toxic relationships:

o everything revolves around satisfying their own needs

o overpowering ego

o selfishness

o sadism

o emotional blackmail

o withdrawal of love

o punishment

o degradation

- belittlement

- making fun of others

- showing no appreciation at all

- assignment of blame

- permanent or recurring criticism

- emotional and physical abuse

- manipulation

- isolation of the victim

- reinterpretation of reality and truth

- lies and false claims

- unclear and contradictory behaviour so that others can never get it right

- "I am the king; all others are my subjects."

- "Gaslighting": the deliberate disorientation and manipulation of the victim, and the promotion of deep insecurity, which gradually deforms and destroys the latter's sense of reality and self-awareness.

There are many other characteristics and variations, but they are all based on the basic pattern of manipulation and belittlement.

## Recognizing Your Own Situation

We don't yet have exact figures on how many people are affected by toxic relationships, and studies are insufficient and few and far between. However, it is essential to understand your feelings and have a clear sense of when selfishness leads to pathological behaviour. That's because, in a web of toxic relationships, those affected have often lost their feelings of trust in themselves, so it is all the more important to seek help so they can honestly and objectively assess their situation.

One thing is clear: No one has the right to harm, restrict, manipulate, or abuse others emotionally, physically, or mentally in any way.

## Disputes and Crises Are Normal

Not every argument and crisis is necessarily an indication of a toxic relationship. Up to a certain point, crises, conflicts, and disputes are normal and necessary. They are part of the process and help us in our common development and our problem-solving endeavours.

In a good relationship it should be possible to genuinely apologize after an argument, and there should be a willingness to work on oneself so that negative behaviour is not repeated.

Conflicts must be resolved in a way that is acceptable to all concerned and, even if the dispute has been heated, solutions should be sought constructively, respectfully, and take place on an equal footing. Whether a relationship can be labelled toxic or not has less to do with the frequency of conflicts and more to do with how all those concerned deal with the particular situation.

Equally, not every emotional injury is a sign of a toxic relationship. No one is perfect; we all come up against our limits from time to time in our dealings with other people. If our own unhealed wounds and traumas from the past are activated, we leave the rational level of the mature, reflective person and fall back into (early) childish behaviour patterns. We lash out wildly and can easily hurt the other person with our words or our behaviour. If we learn from this and look to our own healing, we can heal and forgive old wounds. Our connection to self-love can be substantiated and, over time, we can become a person who is capable of loving and respectful encounters.

When we connect with self-love, we can develop a stable personality.

18

# What Needs to Be Done?

If you realize that you are stuck in a toxic relationship, the first thing you need to do is be honest: Don't lie to yourself anymore or indulge in any more illusions. To help with this, find a neutral person to talk to. It could be a professional therapist or coach or someone close to you whom you trust—someone who won't manipulate you or impose their own solutions on you can help you see your situation objectively. Only when you recognize that you have a massive relationship problem can you start to change things.

Once you have become aware of the problem, it is time to take action. It is essential to have an open discussion with your opposite number, appropriate to the situation, where you can clarify whether they are willing to work with you to find real solutions. In the case of a toxic relationship in a work environment, for example, an external moderator can be brought in; in toxic family systems, family therapy or systemic therapy can help; in friendships, an honest willingness to find a

> Ending a toxic relationship is often the only way to avoid losing yourself completely.

new basis for the friendship is important; and in romantic relationships, couples therapy can help find a solution.

No matter what role you are currently playing in the toxic relationship—victim, perpetrator, or rescuer—the process of freeing yourself from it always starts with you.

The causes of toxic relationships and toxic relationship patterns can always be found stored in our soul and in levels of consciousness that are not normally accessible to us. It is, therefore, essential to free yourself from your own subconscious and intrapsychic patterns; that is, those that take place within the mind, or psyche. Otherwise, we end a toxic relationship, break off contact with our parents, relatives, and friends or quit our job, only to slip back into similar negative relationships and addictions within a short space of time.

This has nothing to do with guilt (see page 48), even though you may feel guilty; instead, it is about genuine inner healing. Blame definitely won't get you anywhere.

## Professional Help

If you realize that you are stuck in a toxic relationship, or several toxic relationships, and you don't have the strength to get out of it yourself, then you should definitely seek professional help from a therapist who is familiar with the problem. It is often only possible to make the leap when fundamental soul issues have been resolved, and access to your own inner wisdom, self-love and self-worth, and inner creative power has been reactivated.

This book and the methods presented in it offer you help and support and aid you in understanding your situation. This may not be enough and you may still not be able to muster enough strength and willpower to free yourself. In this case, the support of a therapist is highly recommended.

## Ego Arises Out of a Feeling of Separation

Our behaviour, especially in relationships, is often shaped by an ego that has arisen from a wounded soul.

A soul entering this world in order to incarnate carries the divine spark of universal, all-encompassing, unconditional love. It understands the nature of the universe and has a specific intention that it wants to realize here on Earth. To do this, it enters into a relationship with the world and other human beings.

In the material world, this soul encounters other energies that are in conflict with its intention, and it is confronted by negative human feelings. This means that the soul is repeatedly hurt by its parents, the environment, and society and slowly loses its connection to all-encompassing love.

Although this love is still stored deep inside, normal consciousness can no longer access it.

These injuries and the lack of connection to love lead to a feeling of loneliness and separation. In order to over-come this pain and no longer have to feel it, the ego is born, which from then on tries to re-establish a feeling of connection through substitute strategies. The inner boycotter—the part of us that derails us again and again and often makes life difficult by putting obstacles in our way—becomes the ego's most powerful ally.

> Soul injuries allow the ego to grow and inhibit our connection to love.

# VICTIMS, PERPETRATORS, AND RESCUERS

In order to understand toxic relationships, it is not enough to point the finger at the supposed "bad guys." Toxic behaviour such as that described earlier is, of course, unacceptable. No one has the right to manipulate, belittle, instrumentalize, or abuse another person to satisfy their own deficits, as happens in toxic relationships.

In this respect, it is essential to set clear boundaries and not tolerate or justify such behaviour under any circumstances.

However, practice shows that there are certain subconscious role patterns that cause some people to stumble from one toxic relationship into the next. To permanently free ourselves from these patterns, we must get to grips with them and with ourselves. So let us take a look at how people act, and what basic patterns they follow.

## The Victim–Perpetrator–Rescuer Mechanism

As long as we carry a wounded ego within us, and this wounded ego is in control, we tend to adopt certain role patterns. In toxic relationships, in particular, we usually find a clear division of roles among victim, perpetrator, and rescuer models.

To be clear from the outset: We are not victims, perpetrators, or rescuers; we only identify with these roles in changing constellations of behaviour. For example, a person may not take on any of these roles at work and act confidently from their inner creativity and wisdom.

When this person meets their parents, however, they may suddenly fall into the role of victim and stoically put up with their parents' belittling behaviour. In their marriage, on the other hand, this person may act as an abuser, disregard the needs of their partner and children, focus primarily on their own selfish interests, and act in an angry and manipulative manner.

Most of the time we don't realize that by unconsciously identifying with these roles, we are perpetuating a nightmare that makes it impossible for us to lead a creative life in freedom and love and build nurturing relationships. The goal here is, therefore, to question your own role behaviour, step out of these roles, and connect with your inner creative power in order to act from an inner state of wholeness and freedom combined with love.

> We identify with the roles of victim, perpetrator, and rescuer in changing constellations.

Let us take a closer look at the individual roles with which we identify in our relationships. Note, however, that they rarely occur in pure form.

## The Role of the Victim

The victim feels powerless and weak. Helpless to do anything about it, they witness time and again how others simply trample over their boundaries. Nobody really takes them into consideration, and all too often their needs are ignored. People in the victim role are repeatedly abused, manipulated, beaten, or humiliated by the perpetrators; they serve as a punching bag for the whims of the "strong." Life doesn't seem to be on their side. No matter what they do, they are the eternal losers. They never manage to succeed at anything.

If a person identifies with this role in a certain area of life, they automatically relinquish all responsibility for their life. It is always the fault of others—their bad parents, their family, the power-hungry colleague, the adverse circumstances, life, or a God who doesn't help them.

The victim recognizes neither their own responsibility nor their own creative power. They don't (yet) know that they are stuck in a role. Recognizing this is the first step towards taking other paths and doing something, despite the difficult circumstances. It then becomes possible for them to heal their soul and leave toxic relationship patterns behind, so that they can shape their life creatively in the future and build fulfilling relationships.

## The Role of the Perpetrator

The perpetrator actually has the same inner emotional problem as the victim; they have just unconsciously decided to adopt opposite life strategies. Cut off from their natural compassion and their true inner strength, they go through life ruthlessly. They are constantly ready for battle and see the earth as a planet where only the strongest survive. They take whatever they want, hurt other people, exploit animals and nature, and are always polishing their winner image.

The perpetrator needs the victim as a counterpart, be it in personal relationships, work relationships, friendships, or within the family. They use people (or even animals or nature) to repeatedly prove their superiority and strength. Especially in relationships with other people, they act ruthlessly and use all possible means of manipulation and degradation just to make themselves feel strong.

If we want to free ourselves from these roles, the path is through healing our soul.

## The Role of the Rescuer

In toxic relationships, it is possible for the rescuer role to be taken on by one of the parties involved as well as by outsiders.

**The perpetrator as rescuer:** The perpetrator, who has just tortured, humiliated, ignored, and degraded their victim, suddenly changes tack and explains that only through them will the victim ever be able to achieve anything. This is an attempt on the perpetrator's part to manipulate the victim's desolate ego even more and make the victim's feeling of self-worth dependent on their goodwill.

**The victim as rescuer:** The victim is trapped in the illusion of being able to get the perpetrator to stop their negative and harmful behaviour. The victim sees it as their mission to save the relationship and is prepared to put up with anything to do so.

**The external rescuer:** The external rescuer sees the problem of toxic entanglement and attempts to help the victim and free them from the relationship. If the rescuer is not caught up in their own helper syndrome, this support can be valuable; however, if the rescuer has helper syndrome and lives it out without realizing that they are no more free than the victim or the perpetrator then, instead of being of help, this complicates the situation further. Since a person with helper syndrome needs someone to help, rescuing the victim is not an option, because otherwise the helper role would become unnecessary and the rescuer would quickly feel useless and empty. Some rescue attempts end in even deeper dependencies and develop into toxic structures themselves, if the basic problem is not recognized.

## The Interdependence of the Three Types

The three basic types—victim, perpetrator, and rescuer—need each other, even if they don't realize it. None of them can exist without the others. By perpetuating this victim–perpetrator–rescuer mechanism, we create our own personal nightmare of envy, resentment, suffering, powerlessness, illness, pain, dependency, weakness, and toxic relationships—day in, day out; year by year.

There are many family systems that also function according to this pattern. The members of the family involved are subconsciously

> Victim, perpetrator, and rescuer are attuned to one another, which makes it difficult for any of them to step out of their role.

assigned certain roles—roles that each of them must maintain in order to keep the balance. If someone tries to step out of their position and role, everyone else involved will do their utmost to prevent it. As a result, many family systems are trapped in their toxic relationship patterns, frozen and unable to act. Blame, taboos, hurts, and unspoken family secrets are maintained, and no one can or is allowed to assume responsibility and thereby, dissolve these blockages in freedom and love.

Certain roles are often passed down from generation to generation. Here are a few examples:

○ The first-born son is supposed to uphold the tradition and carry on the family business, even though he has no interest in doing so.

○ The second-born child plays the role of the black sheep who is not going to adopt the norms and values of the system and who rejects and openly rebels against them.

○ The father is authoritarian and angry, just like his father and grandfather were.

○ The mother is helplessly at the mercy of everyone else's whims, just as her mother was trapped in the role of victim before her.

○ Roles can change in every generation, but if you take a closer look at family systems, it becomes clear, time and again, that certain basic structures exist in every family, and that these are generally passed on to the next generation. All of these roles can be traced back to the victim–perpetrator–rescuer mechanism.

We can also find the same mechanisms in toxic company structures and work hierarchies, in groups of friends and acquaintances and, of course, in romantic relationships.

## The Changing Roles in Toxic Relationships

In some toxic relationship structures, roles are repeatedly reversed, and victims, perpetrators, and rescuers change positions. It is important for those concerned to honestly recognize the underlying structures and their own roles. If we ignore our own part in this, it is often not possible for us to find a satisfactory way out of the dilemma, and we end up in the same structures again and again.

The following example shows clearly how the distribution of roles can change. If one member of the family rebels against the role assigned to them, the whole structure shifts without those involved being able to free themselves from their entanglements.

### The Changing Roles in the Family System

The Smith family consists of father, mother, and two sons. The paternal grandfather lives in the house in a granny flat; the maternal grandparents are deceased, and the sons never met them.

John, the first-born son, is 15 years old and feels *victimized* by the family system. He has to fight for everything that is important to him because his father is very strict and sets tight limits and his mother is anxious and overly protective in wanting to keep her son away from the "evil world." His grandfather always gripes at John when he and his brother are mucking about and playing. It is always John's fault, and his grandfather complains that they are too loud and he can't get any peace and quiet.

As John sees it, his father, mother, and grandfather are the perpetrators. Although his younger brother is almost never held responsible by his parents and grandfather, John sees him as a rescuer, because his brother supports him in arguments with his parents and grandfather and stands by him.

The father also feels *victimized* by the grandfather, his own father. He suffers from the old man's constant complaints, and feels like he has to please everyone, which is impossible. For him, his wife is the rescuer who encourages and supports him and gives him his "tender loving care." He feels he has to set clear boundaries when it comes to his son John, and in this way, takes on the role of perpetrator.

The result of this situation is that John increasingly rebels against his father and his overprotective mother and begins to drink. This shifts the entire role structure. John switches to the role of perpetrator through his aggressive behaviour, spurred on by "rescuer" alcohol, and tries to force his father and mother into the victim role. His brother feels powerless and helpless as a result of this behaviour and also falls into the victim role.

## The Development of the Personality into an Adult State

There is a close connection between toxic relationships, the victim–perpetrator–rescuer mechanism, and the development of our personality. The intentions of our soul and our personality are interwoven.

The healing of the soul must take place first before we can develop our personality into a mature, adult, and sovereign state—only then will there be no more disturbing and blocking impulses from this deeper level of consciousness that prevents the illumination of our core personality, which

We endeavour to develop and liberate the different parts of our personality.

corresponds to us and our true being. We can also see it as part of our life's work to heal, develop, and liberate our soul and personality from any energies that are blocking them.

Let us take a brief look at the different facets or personality traits that shape and define our overall personality. There are three possibilities:

1.  **Inhibition:** Part of our personality is inhibited. We are unable to show this part, unable to live it and, accordingly, quickly find ourselves in the role of victim in this area. We are unable to recognize the underlying inner emotional wounds and deficits, or are so fearful that we don't dare or initially lack the strength to heal them.

2.  **Compensation:** Part of our personality has not been liberated, but we offset this fact by finding a form of compensation for that particular personality area. This usually feels better to us, because the pressure of suffering is not as great as in the case of inhibition. But we are still not living our potential and are not showing ourselves according to our true being and our soul purpose. We play a role and cover up our existing deficits and injuries instead of healing them.

3.  **Liberation:** Part of our personality has been liberated and is no longer subject to any blocking forces. We can live the adult, mature form of that part of our personality and express it in a way that corresponds to our true being and our soul purpose.

Ultimately, it is important to realize the third possibility: to develop the different parts of our personality in such a way that we can live them out in an adult state. This is the prerequisite for getting out of all toxic relationships and relationship patterns, which will then allow us to only form relationships that nourish us, do us good, and enrich us.

The following is a summary of how the first two possibilities are expressed if a part of the personality has not yet developed but has instead been inhibited, or if we are living the compensated form.

- **Real Assertiveness**
  Inhibition: weak on enforcement
  Compensation: aggressor

- **Economic Skills**
  Inhibition: poverty, lack of money
  Compensation: wealth

- **Healthy Communication Skills**
  Inhibition: speech inhibition
  Compensation: constant speaker, waffler

- **Living One's Own Identity**
  Inhibition: lets themselves be cared for
  Compensation: cares for others

- **Healthy Self-Confidence**
  Inhibition: meekness
  Compensation: showoff

- **Ability to Analyze and Self-Criticize**
  Inhibition: is always criticized
  Compensation: the critic

- **Own Taste and Style**
  Inhibition: no personal style, unstylish
  Compensation: particularly stylish appearance

- **Ability to Gain Control over Oneself**
  Inhibition: the oppressed
  Compensation: the oppressor

- **Ability to Create Happiness for Oneself**
  Inhibition: dependent on the happiness of others
  Compensation: the patron, helps others achieve their happiness

○ **Own Rights and Own Responsibility**
Inhibition: the victim
Compensation: always in the right

○ **Ability to Be Free and Independent**
Inhibition: the conformist, the "yes man"
Compensation: the rebel, questions everything and rebels

○ **Ability to Help Oneself**
Inhibition: the helpless person, needs support and help
Compensation: the helper, helper syndrome

If you take a closer look at this list, you will see that most of the traits in the inhibition and compensation list correspond to behaviours that occur in toxic relationships and determine them.

In order to be able to express ourselves and our personality in a mature, adult, healed and liberated form, we must first heal our soul. Unless we do this, the path is often arduous, and many of those who were previously in the inhibited state simply switch to compensation. This usually feels better at first, as there is often less psychological strain and less awareness of suffering and inner emptiness. Unfortunately, this does not correspond to the liberated state and does not free us from the entanglements of toxic relationship patterns and toxic relationships. Liberation is only possible if we develop our personality and live in an adult state.

# PERSONALITY DISORDERS
# AND TOXIC RELATIONSHIPS

Psychology has long endeavoured to define certain personality types that can be used to group people into categories. For example, the victim–perpetrator–rescuer mechanism outlined above can be used to assign corresponding personality traits to people or, using the lists on pages 14–17, to define the personality structures of perpetrators or victims in toxic relationships.

Many toxic relationships involve people with a narcissistic personality disorder.

But the complexity and diversity of being human is clearly opposed to pure categorization. Experience also shows that a wide variety of people with very different personality traits can fall into the trap of toxic relationships—extroverted and introverted, quiet and loud, rational and emotional, young and old, active and passive.

However, according to international classifications, there are certain pathological personality disorders that, due to the resulting behaviour, lead to toxic relationships. This is particularly true of the narcissistic personality disorder, which definitely requires treatment. Relationships with people who suffer from this disorder appear similar to toxic relationships in many respects. In this case, therapeutic help is unavoidable and urgently needed.

# Narcissistic Personality Disorder

People with narcissistic personality disorder—colloquially referred to as "narcissists"— replace their perceived lack of love and support from others by overemphasizing their own value. This disorder not only affects relationships, but often has far-reaching consequences for all areas of life and the narcissist's entire environment.

According to the diagnostic criteria for narcissistic personality disorder as defined by the American Psychiatric Association's classification system (DSM-5), at least five of the following characteristics must be present in order for it to be classified as a mental illness:

1. The person concerned has a terrific sense of their own importance (exaggerates their own achievements and talents; and expects— with nothing to show for it—to be recognized as superior).

2. The person is strongly influenced by fantasies of boundless success, power, splendour, beauty, or ideal love.

3. The person believes themselves to be "special" and unique and only understood by, or only able to socialize with, other special or prestigious people (or institutions).

4. The person demands excessive admiration.

5. The person displays a sense of entitlement (exaggerated expectations of particularly favourable treatment or automatic compliance with their personal expectations).

6. The person is exploitative in interpersonal relationships (takes advantage of others to achieve their own goals).

7. The person shows a lack of empathy; that is, is unwilling to recognize or identify with the feelings and needs of others.

8. The person is often envious of others or believes that others are envious of them.

9. The person displays arrogant, overbearing behaviour or attitudes.

From the description of this personality structure and the comparison with our previous statements concerning toxic relationships, it is obvious that a relationship with a person with a narcissistic disorder almost always contains elements of a toxic relationship.

---

**NOTE**

If you yourself suffer from a personality disorder, or suspect that you do, consult a doctor and have it checked out. In such cases, therapy is absolutely necessary. The insights into the psychological background and the solutions presented in this book can support you on your path, but without professional help it is impossible for you to solve your problems.

---

In shamanism, we assume that all forms of personality disorders have their causes at the soul level, as do all forms of interpersonal conflicts and problems, including all forms of toxic relationships. For that reason, we will now take a closer look at the shamanic concept of the soul, and the shamanic view of the world and the human being, in order to recognize and resolve the underlying causes of toxic relationships.

# 2

# SOUL ISSUES
# AND SOUL WOUNDS –
# THE REAL CAUSES OF
# TOXIC RELATIONSHIPS

One may chop wood, make bricks, forge iron without love,
but one can no more deal with people without love
than one can handle bees without care.

*~ Leo Tolstoy (1828–1910)*

# THE CREATIVE UNIVERSE

If we want to step out of toxic relationships and relationship patterns completely and permanently, we must heal our soul. The soul plays a central role in shamanism. This being so, let us now take a look at consciousness and the shamanic view of the world and human beings.

## Human Consciousness

The principle structure of the universe is pure, unadulterated energy. Colours, tones, sounds, thoughts, feelings, love—everything consists of energy. From all possible forms and variants of energy, the universe is constantly weaving a multidimensional web in which our visible reality materializes. Within this network, everything is connected. Our world is woven into this fundamental vibration and the ongoing creative process of the universe.

Human beings are involved in this creative process with our thoughts, feelings, energies, dreams, actions, and so forth. In this way, we collectively create our reality and our relationships, individually and together. We are usually unaware of this process; however, the more consciously we engage with ourselves and the visible and invisible world, and the more clearly we recognize the laws, the more powerfully and autonomously we can shape our lives and our relationships. It is all about consciousness.

> As part of the universe, human beings are connected to everything and everyone.

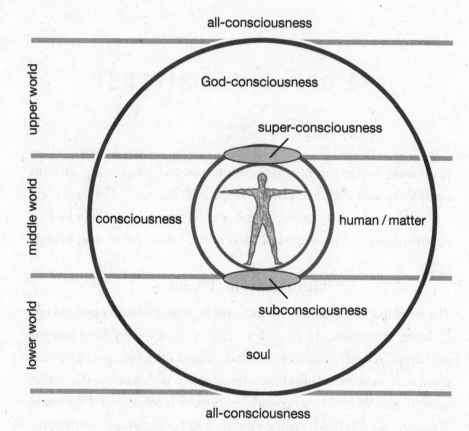

Fig. 1: The Shamanic Model of Human Consciousness

The shamanic model of human consciousness consists of three worlds that comprise a total of four levels. All four levels interpenetrate and are interwoven:

o The ordinary reality of the middle world

o The non-ordinary reality of the middle world

o The upper world

o The lower world

## The Middle World

The middle world lies between the lower and upper worlds and is further divided into two levels: the ordinary and the non-ordinary reality.

o Ordinary reality corresponds to our everyday reality and everything we can perceive within it. This is the level of our normal waking consciousness. This is where we argue with our partner, where we are visibly and tangibly humiliated, and where all toxic behaviour and relationship patterns manifest themselves.

o Non-ordinary reality also exists in the middle world, but we are unable to grasp it with our five senses. It normally remains hidden from us. For example, if you are arguing with your partner, or if you are being insulted and humiliated in a toxic relationship and are perhaps even feeling guilty, then this is your everyday reality. Suddenly, you see a glowing red energy field surrounding your partner or the other person, and within this field there are a great many black dots moving towards you like arrows. This is non-ordinary reality.

o We tend to categorize such perceptions as sick, but for shamans these are normal phenomena. They know that behind the veil of the everyday there lies a world that may often seem irrational at first. Most of the subtle elements of our being are located there, such as the chakras and the aura—in shamanic terms, the soul energy centres and the soul energy fields of human beings.

## The Upper World

In the upper world, our consciousness leaves the limitations of the everyday, visible world. Our super-consciousness resides in a transitional area. Here, we free ourselves from our limitations and connect with our higher self.

The entire upper world harbours the developmental potential of a human being. In it, we find our life plan in coded form and our purpose for this life, with all the dispositions and potentials that we have taken with us into our life on Earth. In the upper world, we find the teacher or spirit guide responsible for our spiritual development and the helping and supporting beings that look after this level.

With a still further expanded consciousness, we immerse ourselves in the consciousness of God. We experience both divine wisdom and ourselves as the creators of our reality.

## The Lower World

In the lower world, our consciousness leaves the limitations of the everyday, visible world. Our subconscious resides in the transitional area. Here, we gain access to all the positive and negative beliefs stored within us that significantly influence our lives and our relationships, and immerse ourselves in the collective level of archetypes and basic psychological patterns.

> Our consciousness is the key to perceiving other levels of reality beyond the material world.

If we expand our consciousness even further, we enter the land of our soul and experience ourselves in our soul landscape. We gain access to the patterns stored within us that underlie our illnesses and our toxic relationships, as well as to our soul guidance.

In shamanic work, the lower world largely corresponds to the "soul garden," an area within us that is home to our archetypes (pages 87–105). Archetypes symbolize partial aspects of our own inner wisdom.

## All-Consciousness

All-consciousness lies beyond the boundaries of our consciousness. When we cross these boundaries, everything dissolves and we experience ourselves as oneness, unlimited love, and All-Consciousness beyond space and time.

This system encompasses far more than our narrow, materialistic view of the world and humankind. These invisible worlds have been known for thousands of years, and shamans, for example, are travellers between the different worlds. Every form of shamanic work takes place on these levels. All levels are of equal value.

With a slightly expanded consciousness—for example, in a shamanic trance, which we can easily achieve in shamanic work by employing a particular drum rhythm (page 125)—we gain access to non-ordinary reality and also to the upper and lower worlds.

## The Shamanic Image of Humankind

We human beings are multi-layered beings and part of the ongoing process of creation in the universe. Through our thoughts, feelings, words, and actions, we constantly send out energy, and thereby contribute to the weaving of the great web. We are therefore co-creators of the greater picture. We are connected to all that exists in this universe via the threads of energy that permeate everything.

In the shamanic image of humankind, there are four areas that make up the human being: body, spirit, soul, and heart.

○ Our body is the vehicle in which we move through this life.

○ Our spirit, our true nature, sits at the wheel and steers the vehicle.

41

○ Our soul is the holdall of our spirit. It contains everything we need
for our path: all the positive and negative experiences we have
ever had, our treasure trove of wisdom, and our connection to
our divine origin as well as to our own inner wisdom and creative
power.

○ Our heart enables us to love others and love ourselves. It connects
us with universal love and acts both as a transmitter and receiver of
this energy.

# The Soul Level

For the most part, we find the true causes of our toxic relationships and
relationship patterns on the soul level. The soul is multidimensional
and is made up of an infinite number of layers. Some of these layers
are particularly important for our shamanic work and for liberating
ourselves from toxic relationships:

○ The soul garden. We enter this level of the soul by means of
shamanic soul journeys (see pages 157–159). It is home to the
archetypes (see pages 87–105), and here we find the stored injuries
and patterns that need to be healed for us to free ourselves from
toxic relationship patterns.

○ The soul energy field – the aura, and the soul energy centres, the
chakras. These areas are described in detail from page 75 onwards.

○ The soul matrix, the spirit matrix, and the teacher/spirit guide
in the upper world. We will not go into this level in detail in this
book.

# Deficits of the Soul that Influence Our Lives

Unnoticed by our normal everyday consciousness, there are fundamental factors on the soul level that significantly influence our lives, our relationships, and our relationship patterns—unfortunately often negatively—and keep us stuck in toxic relationships. We refer to them as "deficits" of the soul to express the fact that there is something lacking. This lack can be remedied; the deficits can be healed.

The following is a list of the issues involved:

o We have no knowledge of the universal, overarching laws of life, and therefore, know nothing about the deeper connections.

o Our emotional access to self-love and self-worth within our psyche is blocked.

o We carry unhealed soul wounds within us. As a result, parts of our soul have been lost and are lacking.

o We are carrying soul parts of other people around with us that we took on or exchanged already before or during the toxic relationship.

o Soul contracts we have made with ourselves or with a partner in a previous life, chain us to toxic relationships.

o In the partnership, we are living out or experiencing the unresolved problems of our ancestors from times long past.

o We have no access to our soul wisdom and our inner self-healing powers.

o We are not following the call of our soul, which means that we are unable to find deeper meaning or satisfying partnerships.

o Toxic relationship patterns, caused by soul wounds, express themselves in disturbances and blockages in our chakras and our aura.

○ Toxic relationship patterns, caused by soul wounds, lead to negative thought patterns and feelings, from which negative beliefs arise. This keeps us trapped in our toxic relationships.

We will look at these issues in detail in this book. You will learn how to recognize them and free yourself from their negative influences. This is how we heal our souls and create the preconditions for fulfilling relationships.

Whether you need to work on all the points listed depends on your current situation and the soul wounds you have suffered in your life so far. To begin with, read everything through in your own time and feel what resonates with you. These are the points you should definitely work with practically.

# THE UNIVERSAL LAWS OF LIFE

According to the shamanic view, and that of many other spiritual schools of thought, human life is governed by superordinate laws. We human beings are subject to these laws, which we cannot change, on all levels of our being. They also play an important role in our relationships.

All cosmic, universally valid laws are timeless. These are fundamental energetic principles according to which our entire universe functions. If you take a closer look at what are called Laws of Destiny, it quickly becomes clear that nothing is left to chance. Conversely, this means that, in harmony with divine will, we are able to determine our own destiny. If we know these cosmic laws and take them into account, they lead us from the powerlessness we feel in the face of (alleged) chance to the freedom of a destiny that we can control ourselves. The most important laws relating to our relationships and our ability to relate are the Mirror Law and the Law of Cause and Effect.

> Knowing the cosmic laws and following them gives us power over our destiny and therefore over our relationships.

## The Mirror Law

The Mirror Law—as within, so without—states that everything we encounter on the outside, in what we call our "reality," only ever reflects what is within us. According to this viewpoint, every encounter and every relationship we enter into in any form, or into which we are born, reflects our own soul themes.

You may be shaking your head indignantly at this point and asking yourself, for example, what your work colleague's aggressive, manipulative behaviour has to do with your inner life, or the behaviour of your mother, who always manages to make you feel guilty and responsible for her well-being. By working honestly with your soul, you will recognize the connections, then your own suppressed anger or your inability to get angry yourself will soon become apparent. Or you will realize that you are still stuck in the role of a child when you are with your mother, and that there are childhood wounds you haven't yet healed.

We generally only identify with the sides of ourselves that we like and try to suppress the dark or painful sides, instead of accepting them as belonging to us and coming to terms with them. But our toxic relationships reflect something that is present within us—something in our soul that is sick and wants to be healed.

Even if we often don't want to admit it, what we encounter and what we resonate with always relates to us in some way, and as soon as we have resolved issues within ourselves and are permanently at peace with them, this is reflected in our relationships and how we resonate with the world around us.

Ultimately, the principle of the Mirror Law drives our development as human beings. The less we have mastered our issues and learning tasks, the greater the friction and the higher the tension. In the most multifaceted ways and on different levels of existence, we then repeatedly draw corresponding events into our lives, with the help of which we can develop and achieve balance. This carries on until we look closely, resolve the issue, make peace, and master the learning task. Inner peace gives rise to inner freedom, and only then are we true masters. Only then do we no longer need the friction and are free to engage in fulfilling, nourishing relationships.

Life will repeatedly test us. It will confront us again and again with different encounters, situations, and challenges in order to check whether we are really inwardly free or just caught up in a new illusion. Once we have developed an adult, mature version of ourselves, the trials cease and the challenging issues disappear from our lives.

People often come to my practice and complain that they have already learnt so many methods, gained so much knowledge, and made so much progress in their development, yet the same problems keep cropping up in their relationships. They are understandably very frustrated.

Such people have often recognized a number of issues already but have simply given up too soon or taken a wrong turn. It may be that they were hoodwinked by a nasty inner boycotter, who tricked them into believing they were on the right path, when the right one led in a completely different direction. The quiet voice of their soul and heart suggested it, but they didn't listen.

Ultimately, it doesn't matter why we haven't reached our goal so far. If it is important to us, then we simply have to set off again, look closely, and be ruthlessly honest with ourselves. This is the only way to recognize why we have not yet achieved success, or made little progress, and are still stuck in toxic relationships.

We need other, more effective strategies—strategies we may have previously rejected, ridiculed, or feared. In that case, we are invited to return to our starting point or the wrong turn and look for new paths that will lead us to success.

Check your toxic relationships and your own toxic behaviour patterns according to the Mirror Law and ask yourself the following: What kind of (life) issue is it that is expressed in your toxic relationships?

## The Law of Cause and Effect

We can rely on the fact that everything we think, feel, say, and do has an effect in the universe, and that we will experience it sooner or later. This makes us co-creators of our reality.

This is where the concept of karma comes into play. We are often unaware of the causes of our toxic relationships and our own toxic relationship patterns, because they date back too far or, if we bring the idea of reincarnation into play, because they lie in previous lives.

We can be sure that we are responsible for everything we experience but should not feel guilty (see the following section). We ourselves have sown the seed, and now it is a question of taking responsibility. In the truest sense of the word, life wants to know what our answer is—an answer that heals us and leads us out of toxic structures, or an answer that keeps us trapped in our dilemma.

Check your relationships and your own behaviour patterns according to the Law of Cause and Effect and ask yourself the following:

o Do you have any memories or ideas about the underlying causes of your toxic relationships?

o To what extent did you contribute to this with your thoughts, feelings, and actions? Or are you even aware that you contributed to this situation?

Clarify for yourself whether these causes are still active and whether you need to change your thoughts, feelings, and actions in order to free yourself from your toxic relationship patterns.

## Guilt and Responsibility

If you are involved in toxic relationships and are either secretly or vocally blaming yourself for it, then please forget about that very quickly. This is never about finding out who is to blame. Feelings of guilt or recriminations don't get us anywhere. The concept of guilt is man-made. It has many social functions and, above all, it makes us feel small and catapults us out of our creative power.

In order to break free from the vicious circle of toxic relationships, we need to put all of our energy into solving and healing the underlying causes, instead of agonizing over questions of guilt. It is important to recognize the situation, understand its deeper message, and make appropriate changes in our lives, our thought patterns, and our relationships. This means we take responsibility for ourselves, and that works.

> It is purely about recognizing the true causes and then healing them within yourself.

We need powerful, lasting solutions so that we don't repeatedly fall back into the same self-loathing, destructive patterns, hooked up with people who don't respect us and only abuse us to satisfy their own narcissistic personality, and through that their own sick, unhealed soul.

Responsibility helps us change our relationship patterns. Guilt prevents this. Ask yourself:

○ Do you feel guilty?

○ Do you feel at the mercy of your toxic relationships?

○ Are you taking responsibility for yourself and your relationships?

## Destiny and Coincidence

Shamans do not believe in coincidence. They assume that we do not meet the people with whom we resonate by chance and that these encounters take place for a specific reason. As explained, everything that happens follows certain laws, which is why we cannot change our basic life plan, our life task, and our purpose (see pages 45–49). However, we are by no means at the mercy of it all. According to shamanic belief, we are in charge of how our lives and relationships turn out—whether we are going to surrender passively, feebly, and powerlessly to whatever happens or powerfully, healthily, and actively live according to our own creative power and shape our relationships.

# THE CALL OF OUR SOUL

The fact that we have incarnated here on Earth follows an inherent soul logic and has a deeper meaning. Our soul knows of this deeper meaning and reminds us again and again that we have linked particular purposes with our life. Through living in relationship with other people, we experience the external mirror that we need in order to see to what extent we are realizing our soul purpose.

Life means development. We can decide for ourselves how this will play out.

We are largely in control of whether we strongly resist our deeper life purpose and go through our lives full of suffering and pain, or whether we follow the call of our soul and grow in the flow of life, full of joy and love. For this, it is necessary to understand the meaning of our existence. In this way, we can align our lives and our goals accordingly, avoid going down the wrong path, and free ourselves from toxic patterns.

## The Meaning of Human Existence

If we know why we are here in this world, and if we orient our lives accordingly by following the call of the soul, it is much easier for us to live our lives in lightness and joy without constantly having to gain experience through suffering. However, it is often only when we are faced with existential decisions, or find ourselves in transitional situations, at the birth of a child, after the death of a loved one, in life-threatening or very traumatic situations, that the big question about the meaning of life arises.

Until we know what it is that makes life worth living, we may cling to our toxic relationships because we fear having nothing else and being alone. Those who have, in general, developed an open attitude and trust in life are much better able to step out of the limited space of consciousness they find themselves in and integrate new experiences into their lives. Those who allow their fears and doubts to dominate them cling to pure survival in their comfort zone. This can quickly become too narrow and turn into an unbearable prison.

### The Question of Meaning

- Do you know why you are here in this world?
- Do you see a purpose in your life?
- Do you recognize a deeper meaning in all your encounters and relationships with other people and in situations and challenges that life presents you with?

Indigenous peoples and tribes who are still integrated into the natural cycles of existence today usually have a clear idea of the meaning of their existence through their traditions, myths, and creation stories. They feel connected to the small and large rhythms of nature and don't question fundamental necessities. Using the self-perception of indigenous peoples and religious scriptures and the problems, deficits, and diseases of modern Western societies with rather questionable, destructive objectives, it is possible to create a picture that depicts the meaning of existence from a higher level.

We are all here to:

o further develop ourselves and our souls;

o master our personal life task;

o fulfil our transpersonal life task as guardians of the earth;

o recognize unconditional love in everything and radiate it outwards;

o recognize and live our life vision and life mission in all of this;

o celebrate life;

o permanently expand our consciousness until we are once again enlightened and at home in All-Consciousness.

Our relationships in all areas of our lives serve to realize this life purpose in all its facets. To do this, however, we need relationships that support and nourish us on our journey and in our tasks. These are relationships that give us the space we need to develop on the one hand, and on the other, take up the life tasks our soul has brought with it, realize these tasks, give them to the world, and enrich life with them.

**The meaning of our existence is also expressed through our relationships.**

We must avoid falling into pure egotism and ruthlessly fulfilling our own needs and desires. We need to take up a sovereign position, similar to that of a king or queen, from which we are able to serve. You need to know who you truly are in order to be able to serve life from a position of inner strength, love, and creative power. In this way, toxic patterns lose their power and everything thrives and grows in love and connectedness for the benefit of all beings.

Clarity is therefore required. You need to be clear about what your relationships mean to you and how you wish to shape them so that they may serve and nourish you and everyone else involved.

## Traveller through Space and Time

We are all on a journey through space and time, and we have already gained a great deal of experience. We incarnate again and again on Earth in order to progress in our development, to familiarize ourselves with the many facets of life and love, and to return home at some point—home to oneness, to our divine home, to pure, pristine love, to All-Consciousness.

Our relationships are a reflection of where we currently stand and how we are doing with regard to our purpose in life. If we are on the way to realizing ourselves and our soul purpose in love, then that is also reflected in our relationships.

> We gain new experiences in every new incarnation. Our relationships help us progress in our development.

## Our Personal Life Task

Our soul has had many positive and negative experiences on its journey through its incarnations. The individual task we set ourselves in this life ties in with all the experiences we have had so far. And of course, it expresses itself in the way we relate to the world and to life.

All of the encounters and relationships we enter into in the course of our lives therefore have the deeper purpose of supporting us in this task and showing us where we currently stand. Life wishes to remind us and shake us awake.

Life asks us these important questions about our personal task in life:

o Why did you come here?

o What do you want to learn and master in this life for your own personal development?

o Are you acting out of deepest love?

o Are you enriching and gifting the world with what you have brought with you?

## Our Transpersonal Life Task

We all belong to the human species and just as there is a personal, individual task in life for each individual, there is also a common, over-arching task for all human beings. Shamans refer to this as "being earth guardians." Let us take a look at our external world: In what way are we looking after and protecting the world, nature and creation? Isn't it much truer to say that in our collective, boundless selfishness we are exploiting and abusing the whole of creation? Our greed for more and more stops at nothing and no one. And we are all involved in this madness through our own personal behaviour. The purpose of our relationships in this context is to enable us to work together on this task.

Life asks us these important questions about our transpersonal task in life:

o Are you serving life or your own selfishness?

o Are you a guardian or an exploiter?

o Are you in harmony with the natural rhythms of life?

o Do you serve life, the world, and nature, or do you behave like a parasite?

o Is your feeling for creation one of love and devotion?

## Love

Love is not rational and cannot be grasped or explained by the rational mind. Love follows no logic, it is simple. We are asked to look with our hearts not with our minds. Through the genuine, deep wisdom of the heart and heartfelt vision, all contradictions and inconsistencies dissolve and merge back into what they ultimately are: an expression of the life

> Love is the building material from which everything is made—creation, the universe, everything that exists.

and love that is behind everything and permeates everything. Love is the basic principle of creation and this universe.

Love leads to inner freedom and expansiveness, to a merging and dissolving of the "I." It is not something you can really give or receive, because love in its true form is simply there, unlimited, infinite. It is available to all beings because it is the basic substance of everything. WE ARE LOVE!

If our awareness of this were omnipresent, and if we were able to grasp the full extent of it, then we would be capable of immediate and boundless love. There is nothing that is not made of love, even if, in the form of a shadow, it may often appear to us to be distorted and evil.

Love, in turn, finds its expression in and through our relationships. If we have internalized the principle of love, then our relationships are automatically more loving.

Life asks us these questions about love:

o Do you see universal love in everything?

o Where in your life are you in judgement mode and therefore in separation?

o Where in your life can you love unconditionally?

## Your Vision and Mission

From all of this, and from your personal and transpersonal life task and the ability to love unconditionally, your personal life vision with all its different aspects grows. If we listen within ourselves, we can hear a quiet voice that shows us the way. If we follow it with confidence, it will lead us to our vision.

From this vision, we can then develop our personal mission and put it into practice. We begin to live our vision. We give the world everything we have brought with us and, in this way, we enrich the world, human beings, creation, and ourselves. We become servants of life and love. And where is this best and most obviously expressed? In our relationships, of course.

Life asks us these questions about our vision and mission:

○ What is your vision of life?

○ How are you turning your vision into a mission?

○ How are you lovingly living out your mission in the world?

## Celebrating Life

Life now becomes a celebration. Through the deep knowledge of our task, the meaning of our life and goal, we shape all our encounters and relationships into a celebration of life and love. We

When we know the meaning of our existence and our vision, we can celebrate life and love.

no longer have to employ tactics, deceive, manipulate, and suffer from the wounded position of the ego, but are able to give ourselves completely to life. Our old, wounded ego burns away in the fire of transformation and makes room for what we always were, always are, and always will be: pure energy—pure, unconditional love.

We no longer attract toxic people into our lives, because we have healed our own toxic structures and soul deficits. At this point, life asks no more questions. We have arrived and, transcending all open questions, we have found the answer within ourselves: LOVE.

# The Goal of Expanding Our Consciousness to Reach a State of Enlightenment

Christianity teaches that after our death, if we live in a seemly way, we will return to God's side, to Paradise, which is described as a place of bliss and oneness.

In Buddhism and Hinduism, enlightenment is seen as the great goal of being human. This state can be achieved during our lifetime and is described as immersion in the All-Consciousness, in which all limitations dissolve and we once again experience ourselves in oneness and infinite love. Our ego, which we normally cling to so tightly, dissolves, and we are immersed in bliss.

> We can decide what is really important to us and organize our lives accordingly.

Where a person directs their energy in life, and what is really important to them, is their own personal decision. However, from the perspective of our soul, if we don't stop orienting ourselves towards unimportant things and wasting our energy in toxic relationships, instead of expanding our consciousness, we shouldn't be surprised if we fail to experience a deeper meaning in life and at some point feel empty, burnt out, exhausted, and ill, and end up stuck in toxic structures.

If, on the other hand, our lives include something that is in harmony with our soul's purpose and that we are inwardly passionate about, then we have something that is worth living for and are prepared to really give it everything in our power. In this way, we can also regard life and all our relationships as the playing field on which we are constantly challenged to expand our consciousness. This certainly does not come about through the accumulation of knowledge but through wisdom. Genuine expansion of consciousness is free of any egoistic motives. To the greater whole, it opens up the space in which we are truly at home: boundless All-Consciousness.

From the shamanic and spiritual view, the only purpose of the time ahead of us is to overcome everything that separates and limits us; to make peace with ourselves and the whole of creation; to be one with all that is; to ultimately immerse ourselves in boundless consciousness once more – or in other words: to unfold our full human potential and return home enlightened.

## Inner Emptiness

Forty-one-year-old Helena had once again separated from a partner. She told us that she had been looking for the love of her life forever. So far, however, her relationships had always been relatively short, and they had all followed the same pattern: To begin with, Helena had had the feeling that she had finally found her dream partner, but it wasn't long before the current partner completely changed their behaviour, withdrew, insulted her, and treated her disparagingly.

While taking a medical history, it quickly emerged that all her previous relationships had contained toxic elements. Helena had ended every relationship in deep disappointment and had set off again in search of her dream partner.

Helena had few friends and no hobbies. She had no idea why she was here on Earth, and she had no idea what she could enjoy doing or how she could make sense of her life other than through relationships. Out of this feeling of inner emptiness, she projected all her hopes of finding happiness and meaning onto a relationship with a man.

During the coaching sessions, it quickly became clear that she had had a lot of imagination as a small child and had been bursting with ideas. But her parents had given this little space. Helena was expected to function within the narrow framework that her parents themselves lived in. "You can forget all that nonsense," she was often told. She learnt to function according to her parents' ideas and adopted them without ever having realized her own impulses, which became increasingly stunted as a result.

We worked intensively on finding meaning as well as discovering and recognizing what could bring her profound, heartfelt joy. This is also how we approached the question of her life task. The more Helena discovered herself and realized that she could lead a meaningful life alone, and the more she followed the call of her soul, the less her previously overpowering desire for a dream partner became.

Helena stopped projecting all her expectations of a happy life onto a relationship. This removed the pressure caused by thinking that her happiness in life was dependent on a man, and she opened up to new relationship patterns and ideas for a truly fulfilling partnership.

# SELF-LOVE AND SELF-WORTH

On the energetic level, our heart is the area within us that connects us with love—with self-love, altruism, and universal love.

Our purpose in life is, among other things, to find our way back to a state of love and to act accordingly. All too often, we forget the person closest to us—ourselves. Self-love is fundamental to getting out of toxic relationships. Until we take ourselves and our real needs seriously and love and accept ourselves, we will always attract people into our lives who precisely mirror this self-rejection.

If we treat ourselves badly, reject parts of ourselves, constantly debase ourselves in our thoughts, reprimand ourselves, insult ourselves, and criticize our supposed weaknesses, why would we expect our partner, our friends, our colleagues, and our family to not do exactly that? It contradicts all logic to think that others should love us unconditionally, that they should treat us with esteem and respect, treat us with dignity and value us unconditionally, if we reject ourselves and are therefore, practically speaking, stuck in a toxic relationship with ourselves.

Self-love is always the first step towards authentic, fulfilling altruism and through that to nourishing relationships, and ultimately, to a universal love that boundlessly loves all of creation.

Self-love does not mean simply putting up with everything you don't like about yourself and the way you behave or the way you think. Instead, it is about lovingly accepting and recognizing that which is. On this basis change is possible, enabling us to work on ourselves and our toxic relationship patterns.

Now the question arises: Do you really consider yourself to be worth freeing from your toxic relationships and toxic relationship patterns?

## Selfishness versus Self-Love

In our society, self-love is all too often confused with selfishness, although the two have absolutely nothing to do with each other. As already explained on page 20, the ego arises from injuries to our soul. The more severe the injuries and the bigger our ego becomes, the more the memory of our divine origin fades. We feel separated and no longer have any connection to all-encompassing love.

We also lose our capacity for self-love, and so our ego takes over and installs substitute strategies, such as the pursuit of recognition, influence, wealth, and fame, or it tries to suppress and manipulate other people as it tries to overcome this feeling of separation and loneliness. It shows no consideration for the needs and feelings of others. Its actions and behaviours are selfish and only aimed at satisfying its own needs without ever reaching its goal. We find these egoistic structures anchored in practically all toxic relationships.

> The ego tries to compensate for the missing connection to All-Encompassing Love with substitute strategies.

No substitute strategy for the missing connection to All-Encompassing Love, however sophisticated, can be truly successful. The only way to overcome this separation is to reconnect with the original Source of Love. We can accumulate wealth, surround ourselves with successful people, achieve top performance, anaesthetize ourselves with addictive substances, manipulate and exploit other people, make ourselves out to be bigger and others smaller, but the emptiness within us will always reappear, until we embark on the path of healing and reconnect with the divine within us.

## Genuine Self-Love

Genuine self-love is based on our connection to the bubbling Source within us, which connects us to our true origin and through this to universal love. At the same time, we need an open, courageous heart that enables us to feel, experience, and pass on genuine love.

If we are capable of genuine self-love, we automatically stop continually feeling small, guilty, imperfect, and inferior. We no longer need to be better than everyone else. We can end the competition and allow ourselves to simply be who we are at this very moment, in love with ourselves—with all our alleged faults and shortcomings. We can embrace ourselves and love ourselves with all our physical and mental shortcomings. Whatever we didn't like about ourselves before is now just allowed to be, is given its place, and we are at peace and in love with ourselves without having to fight or reject anything.

This doesn't mean that we have to accept everything we would like to be different. But it is precisely through fundamentally and lovingly accepting, instead of fighting, that we create the conditions for real, lasting change. We no longer have to waste our energy on a pointless battle with our shortcomings nor expend energy trying to fulfil inhuman expectations coming to us from the outside. We can concentrate on our strengths, and promote and develop them.

Lovingly accepting and recognizing *what is* enables change and opens the door to self-love.

Self-love ends the daily battle with ourselves. It opens the door to our true needs and helps us rediscover our original feeling for ourselves, our body, our mind, and our soul. This enables us to treat ourselves with love and develop strategies for our lives that truly nourish, support, and encourage us. We feel what really does us good, how much sleep we need, what kind of food provides our body with the optimum nourishment, and what kind of mental nourishment our mind needs. We surround ourselves with people who love us for who we are, who are honest with us and don't just suck up to us for selfish reasons. We take time for ourselves and create the life that is truly and authentically ours. We are free and independent of the opinions of others and follow the wisdom within us and the voice of our heart.

## Respect and Appreciation

Were we all in a state of love with open hearts, we would also be capable of authentically respecting and appreciating creation. We would no longer need to be unappreciative of others, disregarding their opinions, views, and needs. We could treat all other beings, including animals and plants, with goodwill and respect their otherness. We would no longer have to put ourselves above others to feel better about ourselves. We could communicate with other people and creation on an equal footing. Because we know who we are and because we love, honour, and respect ourselves unconditionally, we simply no longer feel the need to be better than anyone else. We step out of the competitive mindset and consistently follow the voice of our heart—because we honor ourselves by doing so.

## Forgiving and Letting Go

Unfortunately, our hearts are often closed and we don't feel love; instead, we feel fear, hatred, anger, or rejection. It could be that we were repeatedly hurt or rejected as a child, or perhaps we brought these issues with us into this life, or we may have been repeatedly disappointed when we wanted to open up to others or to the world in love.

To avoid being hurt any further and feeling this pain, which was almost unbearable, we shut down. We separated ourselves from the love within us and buried it under fear, resentment, anger, and rejection.

However, this does not mean that love has disappeared. The good news is that there is no need for us to work for it or earn it in some way. Love is the basic principle and the fundamental energy behind everything. It is always there, within us as well, even if we have lost access to it. The key to regaining access to love is to forgive and let go. We are asked to forgive all those who have hurt us, and at the same time to ask forgiveness of all those people and beings we have hurt. It is essential not to forget ourselves in the process. We also have to forgive ourselves, of course.

> Love is always there—we can regain access to it at any time. The key is forgiving and letting go.

Until we can forgive and let go of old grudges, we remain trapped in negative energies and have no room in our hearts for the love that wishes to flow.

## Excessive Demands and Lack of Recognition

Forty-four-year-old Anja came for coaching because she felt that she "just couldn't cope anymore." A successful naturopath, she was on the verge of burnout. A look at her medical history revealed that Anja had overextended herself for years without realizing it; she had simply accepted her responsibilities as a matter of course.

She was married to a respected lawyer and had two sons, then aged 15 and 17. She lived in a villa with a pool, where she had been caring for her mother-in-law for several years. She had built up her practice on the side when her sons were in primary school. In the meantime, she had at least hired a cleaning lady, but she still did everything else in the household and garden herself.

Anja's sons and her husband had never offered to do any of the work and treated her disparagingly, disrespectfully, and more like an employee than anything else. Her husband had even beaten her several times. He was prone to angry outbursts if things weren't perfect when he got home. Her mother-in-law, who was in need of care, was unhappy all the time and constantly nagged her.

For years, Anja had been busy working, caring, cooking, gardening, shopping, helping her sons with their homework, and so on, all without any recognition from her family. In the meantime, her practice was running very successfully. But here, too, patients kept turning up who showed no appreciation for her work and insulted and abused her when she asked for an appropriate fee for her services.

During the shamanic work, it quickly became clear that Anja had no access to self-love. She had grown up without love and recognition and had deeply internalized the idea that she had to earn both. She had organized her whole life according to this pattern and ignored her own needs, her health, and her limits.

Anja realized that she couldn't go on like that. We worked intensively on her childhood, the lack of love, the exaggerated expectations of her parents, and the associated emotional wounds that had led her to lose access to self-love. After we had taken care of the soul wounds, we reopened this access.

Anja began to recognize herself and her own needs once more. When she finally explained to her family that from now on everyone would have to take care of the food, the house, and the garden and that she would hire a carer for her mother-in-law, she was initially told by everybody, in no uncertain terms, that she was a selfish egotist. But Anja could no longer be manipulated. She listened to the voice in her heart, consistently created more time and space for herself, and in so doing created the conditions for her exhaustion to heal.

# INJURIES TO THE SOUL

It is not only in the shamanic worldview that the soul plays a central role in being human. From our well-being, enjoyment of life, and health to our reason for living, relationships, and relationship patterns, human beings cannot exist without a soul, and injuries to the soul can have serious consequences for our lives. If we heal our soul, we create the conditions for a happy, fulfilled life and relationships.

## Lost Soul Parts

Soul loss—or more precisely, the loss of parts of the soul—always refers to a small section of the soul. Imagine the soul as a sphere. If something happens that is contrary to its intention, a small part of the soul, together with its energy, separates off from this sphere. This is initially a wise mechanism, as it protects the overall energy of the soul. Most separated-off soul parts return to the overall system of their own accord after a short time, when the situation or the cause of soul loss is over.

However, if the injury to this part of the soul is too great, or the memory of the causal event is too traumatic, the part remains separated off and its energy is no longer available to the system as a whole. This creates an energy gap that can manifest itself on a physical, psychological, or spiritual level in the form of symptoms and illnesses. At the level of our interpersonal relationships, this gap manifests itself in the form of false expectations, projections, and longings and toxic relationship patterns within oneself as well as with others according to the Mirror Law (see pages 45–47).

Soul loss can be triggered by any form of traumatic experience, such as a shock, an accident, severe psychological stress, or the loss of a loved one. Soul loss can occur in the womb if the mother, father, or both parents are exposed to severe stress or if the child is rejected. The soul can also be burdened by unresolved karmic problems. But even events that seem less serious at first glance can lead to soul loss, and we often don't remember them at all. When we remain for a long time in circumstances that are traumatic for us and our souls, such as staying in a toxic relationship, this can also lead to one or even several soul losses.

> Injuries to the soul almost always lead to a loss of parts of the soul. When we become aware of the causes and heal them, we become whole again.

Every soul strives for perfection, for wholeness and health. The further a person moves away from this, the greater the likelihood that separation from creation will manifest itself in a loss of soul parts, and subsequently express itself in physical, mental, or emotional symptoms or relationship structures.

Only when we recognize the causes of the soul loss and make peace with them can the parts that have been separated off return to the soul or be retrieved. Wholeness regained at the soul level in this way is the prerequisite for making changes on all other levels of human existence—for becoming healthier, happier, and more satisfied and having happy and nourishing relationships as a result.

## Soul Parts from Other People

It can sometimes happen that we—consciously or unconsciously—take on soul parts from other people or other living beings. We mainly encounter two variants of this:

o **"Voluntary" exchange** of soul parts with people that are close to us, or even living creatures, such as beloved pets. This happens, for example, with married couples who are very closely connected and whose souls are in constant dialogue with each other. Unfortunately, this not only applies to harmonious, loving relationships but also to those that are toxic and emotionally stressful.

o **"Accidental" adoption** of separated soul parts of other people or living creatures, which we initially use to fill an existing soul deficit. This happens, for example, when we find ourselves in exceptionally emotional situations, such as grief, anger, or stress, or when we are not well protected energetically and emotionally. In both cases, we carry foreign energies within us that influence us and unfold their energy in our system. As with the loss of soul parts, this can lead to a wide range of symptoms, put a strain on our relationships and manifest in toxic relationship patterns.

## Soul Contracts that Block Us

You may have made soul contracts with yourself or with other people. They may have come about in this life, but they are often binding agreements within our psyche that extend over many incarnations. We mainly encounter two variants in this case as well:

o **Soul contracts between two or more people.** Positive and negative forms of expression with a binding character give rise to one-sided or reciprocal bonds within our psyche. They can be found in statements such as "I'll love you forever" or "I'll hate you for all eternity." These can become so entrenched that they act like a contract to which all those involved are bound. They must fulfil their part of this agreement until it is terminated. We often enter into relationships with people to whom we are still bound by an old soul contract; for example, from previous incarnations.

o **Soul contracts with oneself.** If we make inner statements such as "I will never fall in love again," "I will never trust another person again," or "I will never be happy again" in emotional situations, such as accidents, break-ups, experiences of death, or toxic relationships, this can also lead to a soul contract with a correspondingly binding effect. We then fulfil this contract until we recognize it at some point and dissolve it. If the corresponding contract affects our relationships, our ability to relate to others will be impaired and develop in the way the contract specifies. According to the basic law of resonance, we then automatically attract people whose behaviour subconsciously ensures that our relationship with them is toxic, in accordance with our soul contract.

Some people avoid consciously severing such ties at the soul level if these soul contracts concern people with whom they are in close contact or entangled in toxic relationships. They are afraid that the resulting freedom will change their lives and result in losing people they have been close to.

Be aware that this can happen, but by now, you should have realized that any form of dependency in a relationship obstructs the path to inner freedom and healing. Healing is essential if you really want to live a healthy, authentic, and self-determined life. A relationship based on coercion and dependency can never make you truly happy. It creates suffering, misery, and illness.

> Soul contracts often bind us to people with whom we are entangled in toxic relationships.

## The Consequences of Soul Wounds for Our Lives

If the missing soul parts are not retrieved and existing soul contracts dissolved, this can have serious consequences for our lives, our well-being, our development, our ability to relate, and our relationships. We constantly lack energy, we feel neither complete nor well, and we may even become chronically ill. We repeatedly find ourselves in difficult conflicts that do not resolve. We are unable to make progress in certain areas of our lives, and everything ends up revolving around us and our problems. We disregard the legitimate needs and demands of our fellow human beings and fall in with narcissistic people and have toxic relationships.

As our society usually lacks knowledge when it comes to the soul and its potential problems, and no in-depth solutions are readily available, many people develop narcissistic traits themselves. Instead of gaining access to their subconscious minds and soul consciousness, understanding intrapsychic connections, and creating appropriate solutions, they become self-involved, get nowhere, and gradually take themselves more and more seriously.

Another variant consists of coming into contact with narcissistic people in our environment. Through their behaviour, they act as a mirror and show us that we, too, are inwardly self-involved and stuck in our search for solutions. The less aware we are of our emotional deficits and the more we have given up on ourselves internally, the stronger the narcissistic manifestation can become in our immediate environment.

## Lost Soul Parts

John, 31, and Karin, 29, who had been married for four years, came to the coaching session together. They had a toxic relationship with changing roles. They insulted, humiliated, and manipulated each other with increasing intensity. After both of them became violent, they decided to try therapy. In the initial medical history interviews, they both showed slightly narcissistic personality structures.

The following picture emerged during the shamanic work: John had lost three parts of his soul. The first had already departed before his birth, when his father had urged his mother to have an abortion and had left her when she had decided to have the child. The second part left when he was about three years old, when his mother spoilt him excessively on the one hand and humiliated him on the other. She had no job and no new relationship and forced her son into playing the role of her little prince. He got everything he wanted, unless he failed to behave in the way his mother wanted, in which case she insulted him, calling him "his hateful father's freak," degraded him, humiliated him, punished him, and blamed him for her misfortune. The third part of his soul left when John started school at the age of six and initially experienced nothing but teasing and bullying.

Karin had lost two parts of her soul. The first left when her mother died in childbirth. The second left at the age of five, when her father sexually abused her after treating her like a princess for years and showering her with gifts.

John and Karin were also connected by a soul contract through the words "Our relationship is eternal," a bond they had formed in a previous life. After John and Karin had retrieved and integrated their missing soul parts and the soul contract had been dissolved by both of them, we were able to work on their relationship patterns, and they learnt to treat each other with respect and esteem in a completely new way.

# THE RELATIONSHIP PROBLEMS
# OF OUR ANCESTORS

Toxic relationships and entanglements can also be found in family systems. These behavioural patterns are often passed on from one generation to the next. This means that relationship problems that are rooted in the system can go back seven generations. In this case, we live and repeat the relationship patterns of our ancestors that have never been questioned or healed.

In a shamanic context, we regard our ancestors as an energy field into which our soul is born, because the vibration of our own soul resonates with the vibration of the respective family system. This ensures that the soul is given the optimum environment in which to further its development, take the necessary learning steps and overcome any blockages. Unfortunately, this does not only include positive energies and patterns. Negative, blocking patterns, our own toxic relationship patterns, and our resonance with toxic relationships all form corresponding resonance fields as well. This means that we also find our own negative patterns anchored in the energy field of our ancestors in previous generations.

In therapeutic work, it has been impressively demonstrated time and again that working with the energy field of the last seven generations can be of great help in healing our souls and freeing us from our toxic relationships. We receive decisive impulses to enable therapeutic blockages to disappear and self-healing to take place with full strength and vigour. Anyone who has been burdened by massive family problems will be able to understand that resolving these conflicts can make a fundamental contribution to the healing process.

## Problematic Patterns in Family Systems

Mark, 22, came to the practice because, on the one hand, he could no longer stand living with his family (his mother and an older brother) and wanted to move out, but on the other, he felt obliged to continue working on the dairy farm. He suffered massive feelings of guilt for even considering "abandoning" his family, as he put it. His mother was hot-tempered and angry. He had grown up with beatings and humiliation. As a child, his mother had often locked him in their dark cellar for several days if he hadn't done his chores as she expected. His older brother treated him in the same way as his mother, and he was also repeatedly abused by his older brother, especially as a child.

After completing a few other therapeutic steps, we turned our attention to his family system. Both his brother and his mother subconsciously projected onto Mark the anger of having been abandoned and let down by the father of the family. Mark's father had run off with a younger woman shortly after his birth. We also found this pattern of the "husband and breadwinner abandoning the family" in his great-grandparents' generation: His mother's grandfather had been killed in the war and her grandmother had been left alone with the farm and five children. In the fourth generation previous to Mark's, the then current farm owner had died due to severe alcohol abuse and had also "abandoned" his wife and six children.

This pattern had become ingrained in the family **system** and had been unconsciously passed on from **generation** to generation. Mark worked with this pattern using **the** 7-generation constellation and, on behalf of all **those** involved, carried out the necessary act of forgiveness. **This** enabled the originally powerful energy of the family **system** to flow again. He freed himself from his feelings of **guilt and** was finally able—surprisingly, with his mother's **consent**—to go his own way and leave the farm.

# OUR SUBTLE ENERGY SYSTEM

The human subtle energy system, like everything else in existence, is multi-layered and multi-dimensional and consists of various components. Let us look at the aura and the chakras and how they relate to our soul and our relationships.

The soul expresses itself in non-ordinary reality (see pages 38/39) via the chakras and the aura, the energy centres in the body. Through these, it enters into contact with the world and absorbs subtle energies. If we wish to connect in the most favourable way with our environment in all areas of life and to interact with it, it is necessary for our chakras and aura to function without restriction. If there are disturbances, blockages, weaknesses, or even excess energy, then this exchange no longer functions optimally, which leads to states of either lack of energy or excess energy.

Weak or blocked chakras, a weak, blocked aura, or too much energy in these areas can result in physical, mental, psychological, spiritual, and energetic problems. This can affect almost all areas of life. Conversely, problems in other areas of our existence can lead to blockages and weaknesses in our chakra system and in our aura. In this way, everything is interdependent and in mutual interaction, revealing the fundamental problems of our existence on different levels.

Our relationships, in which a permanent exchange takes place on all levels, have a direct and immediate influence on the state of our subtle energy system.

# The Aura – the Soul's Energy Field

Our aura surrounds us like a shell. Imagine a person surrounded by a colourful, cloud-like structure made up of several layers, roughly in the shape of an egg. This energy structure is not static but pulsates, expands, contracts again, and glows in different colours that change, depending on the mood and condition of the person. The aura extends between 30 centimetres and 1 metre around the body.

*The aura constantly changes its colour, shape, and extent, subject to our changing and constantly shifting streams of thoughts and feelings.*

Our aura connects us with all the forces and energies that surround us and at the same time provides us with a protected space, an energetic space of our own. At the outer edge of our aura, a permanent exchange between our own energies and the forces surrounding us takes place.

Every form of blockage, problem, or injury leaves a mark in our aura and is stored there. In such areas, the energy flow slows down, speeds up, or is frozen. The colour there is usually significantly altered or faded.

## The Aura as an Energetic Filter

An energetically stable aura is essential for us to feel good and stay healthy, or become healthy once more. It is able to intelligently and wisely decide for us which of the forces around us are good for us and which are harmful. Ideally, our aura works like a filter that only lets in what is good for us, strengthens us, and helps us significantly, and at the same time, only allows those of our own energies that are good for and support the world around us to be sent out. For this to work well, it is necessary for us to maintain, promote, or restore the free flow of energy in our aura.

# The Chakras – Our Soul Energy Centres

The best-known chakra system comes from Indian philosophy. According to that, there are seven main chakras along our spine that connect the crown of the head with the lowest point at the coccyx.

The energy that flows in and out through the chakras is distributed via the aura. In this way, our aura is in constant contact with the world and beings around us, and is also in direct contact with our soul via our chakras. Accordingly, our soul garden is connected to our aura via our chakras; in other words, to the soul energy field via the soul energy centres.

## Chakras, Body Areas, and Personality

Each chakra is assigned to different organs and areas of the body and is related to certain basic human personality and personality development themes.

Disorders can lead to a variety of complaints in the associated organ systems and have a strong influence on the corresponding life themes. Our chakras are, of course, also confronted with the corresponding negative energies of all forms of toxic relationships, and they can be weakened or their function can be impaired as a result.

## Blockage of the Heart Chakra and Shortness of Breath

Sandra, 33, was single and worked in customer service in a large company. She was well liked by customers, but that didn't stop her direct superior from constantly criticizing her and regularly making a point of telling all her colleagues and customers that she should try harder and wasn't doing her job well.

Both customers and colleagues repeatedly confirmed to Sandra that she was doing her job well and reliably. But whenever she was criticized by her superior, Sandra felt as if "armour plating was being put around her chest." Her entire chest often felt as if it was in a constrictive corset for hours afterwards, sometimes for several days. She had more and more frequent attacks of acute breathlessness, until she finally ended up being taken to the emergency room at her local hospital. No organic cause was found during the examinations.

Shamanic work with her aura and her chakras revealed that there were dark spots in her aura in the area of her ribcage that were obstructing the flow of energy. These blocking forces were regularly activated when she had problems with her superior. They then spread out like a ring in her aura and led to a blockage of her fourth chakra, her heart chakra. This was the cause of the physical symptoms. We worked with her aura and the blocking forces and, of course, also with the underlying causes on the soul level that had led to Sandra having a toxic relationship with her superior in the first place. This had to do with an old, unresolved problem with her mother that Sandra had had as a child. Sandra was experiencing the same pattern with the same symptoms once again with her superior.

After the causes on the soul level had been healed and we had released the old, childhood blockages, as well as those forces that were currently blocking her aura, Sandra was able to firmly stand up for herself for the first time.

She sought help from the employee representative. The supervisor was transferred, and Sandra's new boss was well disposed towards her and appreciated and valued her work.

# Supportive Universal Forces

We all come from Oneness, wherein there is no separation, only connection, pure love, and unity. Out of this Oneness, polarity is born and created throughout the material world. Everywhere we go, we encounter supposed opposites that together represent Oneness: light and dark, day and night, man and woman, good and evil, and so on.

In the shamanic world view, it is essential for us to have a stable connection with all the positive forces around us that support, nourish, promote, and protect us and accompany us with their wisdom. Our subtle energy system establishes these connections with all the subtle energy fields around us.

The two most important energy fields directly symbolizing polarity are the energies of Mother Earth and Father Sun. These two forces connect us directly with the primordial masculine and feminine poles, which spring from Oneness. Externally, they represent the fundamental polarity that characterizes life in this world.

> A stable connection to positive forces and energies is important.

A good connection to the supportive forces of Mother Earth and Father Sun is fundamental to everything we do in life. If there are disturbances in this area, our most elementary connections—those which give us support and stability and enable us to orient ourselves in the world—are impaired. Negative energies cannot be neutralized and released. They accumulate or enter our environment via our energy system, which in turn has negative effects on our relationships.

## Lack of Earthing

Tom, 72 years old, married with two grown-up children, came to the practice because he had severe pain in his lower abdomen. Conventional medical examinations had not found anything. The medical history interview quickly revealed that almost all of the relationships in his life up until then had been characterized by toxic elements.

With his irascibility and his arrogant, overbearing, and manipulative personality, he conveyed to the people around him that they were useless and that only they were to blame if something went wrong.

And a lot had gone wrong in Tom's life, as he told me. His children had broken off contact with him, his wife had recently left him, and he had been let go from jobs several times after starting arguments with work colleagues. He had been forced to hand over his driving licence a long time ago, after several drink-driving incidents.

Tom initially saw no connection between the pain and his toxic personality structure. However, it soon became clear that his connections to the energy field of Father Sun and Mother Earth were almost non-existent. His earthing ability—the ability to connect to the spiritual forces of the earth, which ensures a natural discharge of negative energies—was completely blocked. This resulted in his toxic, negative energies building up inside him and then discharging abruptly and without warning.

We started by working with these basic upward and downward connections and with the soul wounds from early childhood that had led to these disconnections. The pain soon subsided. Tom became calmer and more balanced.

# THE ENERGY OF THE
# FOUR ELEMENTS

The description of the four elements—fire, earth, water, and air—is based on the teachings of various Greek philosophers who attempted to explain the nature of human beings. This concept can also be found in many shamanic cultures. It provides a comprehensive understanding of the interplay of energies in all living beings. Ultimately, all known occurrences and phenomena on the energetic level are a result of this interaction of the elements.

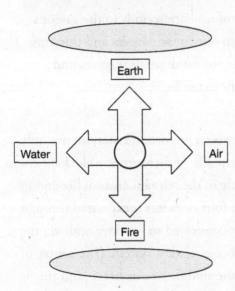

Fig. 2: The Four Elements with
the Heart at the Centre

The four elements are four immaterial forces that exist within us from which we shape our entire life in the visible world and, through this, our relationships and their quality. You could also say that they supply everything within us on all levels of our being with the appropriate energy for manifestation to take place in the world. Our heart, as a spiritual entity of love and as the energetic centre of the energies of the four elements, plays a decisive role in this.

81

○ **The element of fire**, behind us, corresponds to all the energetic aspects within us and also our will. It is the power that supports us from behind and gives us the energy we need to go through life. Fire is the fundamental energy that enables us to act and realize our dreams and intentions.

○ **The element of earth**, in front of us, corresponds to the material aspects within us. It is the densest element. The path of life leads forward and, in front us, our life is realized in the form of matter—earth forms matter and connects us with physical existence.

○ **The element of water**, to the left of us, corresponds to the fluid aspects within us as well as to our sensations and feelings. It accompanies us with the ability to feel and sense. Water gives all our actions and thoughts an individual colour through this connection to our feelings.

○ **The element of air**, to the right of us, corresponds to the gaseous-volatile aspects in us, as well as to our consciousness and thinking. It accompanies us with the ability to think, analyze, plan, and reflect; in other words, the ability to use logic.

The free flow of the elements' energy is an important criterion, not only for our relationships but for our entire life. If there are any blockages or energy deficits, this shows up directly in the relevant areas of life and in our relationships. The power of the four elements is expressed through our heart and is, therefore, directly connected to self-love and, via the fourth chakra (the heart chakra) to our chakra system. The centre of the four axes is located exactly in the middle of our heart, and this is also where our sacred space opens up within (see page 81).

Every human being is born with a certain percentage distribution of these elements that supports our soul's intention in the best way possible and helps determine how we relate to life. Over the course of our lives, this distribution repeatedly changes and adapts to our situation. Things become problematic when individual elements are blocked or weakened, resulting e.g. in another element having a surplus of energy. The aim is

> Every form of illness, malaise, and toxic relationship and relationship pattern can be traced back to a disturbance in the energy of the four elements.

to release and heal energies that block and weaken and to avoid lingering in one single element. Only when we are freely connected with all four elements from the centre of our heart are these forces available to us, without limitation, for our lives and our relationships.

## Blocking of the Four Elements

Duality is the underlying principle of the material world. To enable the infinite diversity of life, this principle was differentiated into four parts in a subsequent step of creation: the four elements. Depending on which element is weakened or blocked—usually due to deep soul wounds—there is a corresponding effect on our relationships.

o **If the element of fire is affected,** we lack the necessary energy to even begin to implement our ideas, plans, conceptions, wishes, and desires with regard to our relationships. We get stuck in our thoughts and feelings and are unable to take action.

o **If the element of earth is affected,** we are limited in our ability to take the step into the material world. No matter how hard we try, we achieve only unsatisfactory results in the material world, or none at all. Whatever we do, we are unsuccessful. Our toxic relationships and relationship patterns persist, and we are unable to take any steps towards healing.

○ **If the element of water is affected,** all our results are unsatisfactory, because they are not in keeping with our nature and our true attitude towards life. Everything we do feels foreign. We have no access to our true feelings, and therefore, no change we feel comfortable with in our relationships.

○ **If the element of air is affected,** we lack the clarity we need to make plans and use them to design a strategic structure for our projects. We get bogged down and make unnecessary mistakes; everything seems chaotic, and the results don't match our original intention. We have no understanding of our relationships, and are chaotic and disorganized in that respect, too.

But even if the four elements are free of blockages, this doesn't mean that their energy is flowing harmoniously within us. We are all more or less influenced by the external forming of our character and don't realize it. We often adopt positions that are not in keeping with the wishes of our soul. Our ego makes us believe that this is who we are. We can only heal our soul and any blocking energies if we recognize that these are foreign programmes and views that our subconscious has internalized, and by which we are being influenced.

This programming causes some people to reject certain elements and favour others, although their natural temperament is quite different. For example, if we grew up in a family where things were always rational and feelings not shown, we may have simply adopted this pattern, even though the element of water is particularly strong in us. The energy of water is experienced as a threat and is rejected, and we behave accordingly in our relationships. In this case, there is no direct blockage of the element, but an excessive

> Foreign programming leads to a disturbance in the composition of the energies of the elements that would be natural to us.

amount of the element of air is used as a substitute. To establish a harmonious form that accords with us in such cases, we walk the entire path of soul healing, freeing ourselves from false and toxic patterns.

## A Strong Water Element Weakens the Fire Element

Hanna, 33 years old, single, no children, came to the practice because, in various relationships, she was invariably drained of all her energy in a very short time. This led to her being insulted, reprimanded, and sometimes bullied by the people concerned.

She suspected that she was being "energetically sucked dry" by others, so she had ended relationships, given up friendships, and changed jobs several times. She no longer dared to engage with people and felt she was becoming paranoid and crazy. She became increasingly suspicious and cautious of other people, and over time, she isolated herself more and more.

The shamanic work revealed that her ability to separate herself was well developed and that the problem was to be found on the level of the four elements. The main problem was that the fire element was greatly weakened by the water element as soon as a relationship began to solidify in the material world (earth element).

The more concrete the manifestation of a relationship, the stronger parts of the element of water became (in this case subconsciously stored feelings of fear of relationships) and these then increasingly "extinguished" the fire—the energy that was necessary to maintain and deepen the relationship—until it was extinguished. This corresponded to her state of complete lack of energy. Her subconscious relationship fears were then projected onto the other person until they, at some point, displayed toxic behaviour and Hanna ended the relationship.

We worked with the four elements in various rituals and journeys and explored those relationship fears expressed in the element of water. Once the causes from her childhood had been resolved and the water element had been freed from fears, the fire element was able to fully unfold its power, Hanna remained in her power and energy, and was able to begin shaping and living in relationships that suited her.

# ARCHETYPES –
# PRIMAL IMAGES OF THE SOUL

Archetypes are primal images of the soul. They dwell in our soul garden and work from there for our benefit. Fundamentally, these are entities that, in their basic energetic form, are present in every soul and thus, can be found in all human beings. At the same time, they are closely linked to the individual's personal history and intrapsychic emotional development. This is why they appear in each person in their own unique, individual form and manifestation.

In their entirety, these soul archetypes embody our soul wisdom, which expresses and shows itself through them. They don't work for our well-being in isolation but are all interconnected. If we come to them with a problem—for example, a relationship problem, an illness, or diverse symptoms—they work closely together and help us to solve the problem and heal. They not only help us with problems but, when we establish a connection with them, also accompany us in our everyday lives.

Through shamanic journeys we can connect with our archetypes and then learn more about the intrapsychic difficulties that underlie our problems. With their help, we can gain knowledge and find solutions to our problems.

A solution on the soul level is always the prerequisite for resolving our relationship problems in life. By activating our archetypes, their (our) wisdom begins to create possible solutions. We connect with our

During shamanic journeys we connect with our archetypes. With their help, deep healing work takes place.

own inner wisdom and creative power, and this makes change possible.

This contact with the respective archetypes is what enables the actual healing of the soul to take place. Each archetype is especially attuned to certain areas of life and situations. They clearly show us which psychological issues are causing us problems.

## The Archetypes

○ **The Power Animal** is our tour guide on all our soul journeys. It knows which other archetypes can best help us.

○ **The Source of Life** connects us with the primal source from which our primal trust is nourished and, furthermore, with the primal force of the universe.

○ **The Inner Warrior** is responsible for our ability to set boundaries. The Inner Warrior makes sure that we can create and maintain a personal space in keeping with our nature.

○ **The Place of Power** connects us with our own inner soul power. There, we can recharge whenever needed.

○ **The Inner Teacher** helps us with advice when we need support with important life issues.

○ **The Inner Healer** is responsible for activating our self-healing powers, for maintaining health and healing.

○ **The Blacksmith** watches over our relationship lines and makes sure that they are cleared or severed if necessary.

○ **The Fire of Transformation** is the place within our psyche with the greatest power of transformation and where encounters take place.

o **The Heart Warrior** connects us to our heart's fire and accompanies us on our path to our purpose in life.

o **The Transition into the Light** is the place where everything finally comes to an end and where we are shown the way after our death.

o **The Rock of the Ancestors** connects our individual soul with the energy of our ancestors.

o **The Mountain of Visions** helps us recognize our life task and purpose and develop visions for our future life.

o **The Inner Man** reflects the masculine side within our psyche.

o **The Inner Woman** reflects the feminine side within our psyche.

o **The Lovers** show us the connection between our masculine and feminine sides and connect us with our creative power.

o **The Inner Child** is the essence of the connection between the Inner Man and the Inner Woman and connects us with the playful part of ourselves.

## The Most Important Archetypes for Healing Toxic Relationship Patterns

In our souls, we have stored all the archetypal forces that connect us with the collective primal themes of being human. When it comes to our relationships, the interplay of all these archetypes is important. The most important archetypes, those that reflect our own ability to relate to others and that work together to show us the state of our relationships and what we need to change, are the archetypes of the Inner Man, the Inner Woman, the Lovers, and the Inner Child.

We all carry these intrapsychic forces within us. Each archetype has a particular colouring, depending on what we have experienced in relation to the themes of the individual archetypes, both in this life

In the context of toxic relationships, we will look in more detail at the Fire of Transformation, the Inner Man, the Inner Woman, the Lovers, the Inner Child, the Inner Warrior, the Inner Teacher, and the Blacksmith.

and in previous incarnations. From deep within, this determines our self-image and perception of people in the world around us and determines how we act in our relationships and who we attract into our environment. If there are any blockages, or if this image is clouded, distorted, or not really tangible, then, using the power of the soul and subconscious, it knocks again and again to remind us that something is running at less than its full power and strength, and therefore, the corresponding potential cannot be lived to its full extent.

Please note that the following archetypes are inherent in all of us, regardless of gender. Everything in this world has two poles: light and dark, man and woman, lover and beloved. We all, whether man or woman, always incorporate both poles. Within their psyche, everyone, whether man or woman, is therefore both lover and beloved, father and mother, sun and moon.

We tend to identify with only one pole, the one that corresponds to our self-image and our identification with one gender. From the perspective of the soul, however, it is always a question of recognizing, understanding, and mastering both poles of reality. In all our relationships, we are constantly encountering the opposite pole externally, which gives us the opportunity to recognize and realize these sides of ourselves.

## The Inner Man

This archetype fundamentally embodies the masculine pole of duality in our soul. It reflects our own interaction with this pole and connects us with the power of Father Sun. Depending on our life theme, it expresses itself through different facets of its being: the King, the Warrior, the Beggar, the Monk, the Lover, the Creator, and so on.

Our Inner Man can be inhibited in his strength, he can compensate for his deficits or, in his adult form, be sovereign in his power and strength.

Depending on the experiences stored within our psyche and the personality patterns we have brought with us into this life, our Inner Man reflects our own unique male approach to relationships. Through his actions, likes, and dislikes, and through his intrapsychic behaviour, he shows us how we approach our partners, what we desire from a relationship, and how we are seen by our partners in relation to our male pole. It is the masculine energy that manifests itself outwardly and in relationships.

The Inner Man represents our interaction with the primal masculine pole of this universe, our interaction with masculine leadership, the father figure that acts as a role model, and protects, safeguards, and demonstrates the masculine aspect of dealing with life.

> The Inner Man connects us with Father Sun, the Inner Woman with Mother Earth.

Another aspect is masculine giving and creative power, which combines with the feminine elemental power in the act of sexual union to create new life.

## The Inner Woman

This archetype fundamentally embodies the female pole of duality in our soul. It reflects our own interaction with this pole and connects us with the power of Mother Earth. It expresses itself through different facets of its being, depending on our life theme: the Queen, the Warrior, the Virgin, the Lover, the Creator, the Saint, the One in Need, and so on.

Like the Inner Man, the Inner Woman can also be inhibited in her power, can compensate for her deficits or, in her adult form, be sovereign in her power and strength.

Depending on the experiences that are stored within our psyche and the personality patterns we have brought with us into this life, our inner woman reflects our own unique feminine approach to relationships. Through her actions, likes, and dislikes, and through her intrapsychic behaviour, she shows us how we receive and accept our partners, how we are able to give ourselves to another, and how we are seen by our partners in relation to the feminine pole within us. It is the feminine energy that manifests itself outwardly and in relationships.

The Inner Woman represents our interaction with the primal feminine pole of this universe, our interaction with feminine leadership, the mother figure that acts as a role model, and nurtures, provides, shelters, and demonstrates the feminine aspect of dealing with life.

Another aspect is the feminine, receptive, creative power, which connects with the masculine elemental force in the act of sexual union to create new life.

## The Lovers

The archetypes of the Inner Man and the Inner Woman give rise to the archetype of the Lovers. This clearly shows how well these two archetypes are functioning, where our energies are flowing freely, where our deficits are, how these two archetypes are working together in relationships and in love, and how matters stand with regard to our inner creative power.

This is where it becomes clear that it is not enough to just heal our masculine or feminine side. Only when both sides are released, free, and whole, do our previous toxic relationship patterns and restrictions dissolve. This, in turn, is then expressed in fulfilling, nourishing relationships and our creative power, which shapes and enters into self-determined, sovereign, and free relationships for the benefit of all.

# The Inner Child

If the Inner Man and the Inner Woman are sovereign in their power, strength, freedom, and ability to love, a wonderful, powerful, and loving archetype of the lovers emerges from the unification of the two. From this, in turn, our Inner Child is constantly reborn and nourished.

Here we can see how important it is to free ourselves from all past injuries and entanglements that have previously influenced our Inner Child and prevented it from coming into its own. If our Inner Child has not been hurt and can act freely, then it has one single, genuine desire: It wants to play. Watch a healthy, happy, little child at play. They are completely immersed, with great seriousness, in their playing; they are in the here and now, completely present in the moment. As long as basic needs such as hunger, thirst, tiredness, or the need for closeness don't become more important, the child will happily carry on playing.

> The Inner Man and the Inner Woman merge in the archetype of the Lovers, which creates the Inner Child through its creative power.

This aspect of play is hugely important in all relationships and for living in love. If we all did as the child does, then we would prioritize "playing together" and would treat each other with love and respect as we play. We would be in the moment in every encounter and free from all negative experiences. We would not project our problems onto these encounters and would experience them as being real and authentic.

This is where these four archetypes come full circle: When the Inner Child is in its own power, love, and freedom, its ability to play in the here and now has, in turn, an effect on the Lovers, resulting in positive feedback to the Inner Man and the Inner Woman. In this way, these four intrapsychic forces within us are interdependent, and we are called upon to do everything we can to enable them to find their true inner greatness and, shining and radiant, unfold their full power and love.

# Toxic Masculinity and Femininity

If our masculine and/or feminine principle is injured and carries toxic structures within it, this also manifests in our intrapsychic state via the archetypes of the Inner Man and the Inner Woman. No unification takes place, and our Inner Child is in a deficient state. Furthermore, we are incapable of fulfilling our transpersonal life task as earth guardians; we can neither celebrate nor honour life and nature, nor can we protect them. We are separated from the cycles of nature and natural growth and unable to fit into the cycle of nature's emerging and eventually passing away. Natural growth is replaced by artificial and material growth.

But the madness of eternal growth in the material sphere has proved to be a dead end. The basis for this is a patriarchy that demonstrates an exaggerated toxic male principle. As a result, a ruthless, sick, and destructive principle determines our actions. This, in turn, is based on the sick, blocking patterns of our unhealed and wounded soul.

Toxic masculinity and toxic femininity lead to separation from the natural cycles of life.

Unless we begin to overcome this patriarchy in ourselves and our souls, we will be unable to find a way to free our relationships from toxic patterns. We are, therefore, called upon to heal our inner masculine and feminine sides, to harmonize them, and thereby reintegrate ourselves into the natural cycles of life—in other words, heal our own inner nature and honour, guard, and protect it.

## Toxic Masculinity

If our Inner Man is trapped in the structures and energies of toxic masculinity, he wants to dominate, exploit, and subjugate the feminine principle. He is not prepared to recognize it as an equal. The idea of honouring and protecting the feminine principle in its liberated form, and opening a space in which it can grow and flourish in harmony with the masculine principle, is met with incomprehension by the toxic masculine principle. It is repressed and ridiculed, triggering states of anxiety.

## Toxic Femininity

If our Inner Woman is trapped in toxic femininity, she neglects her natural feminine principles, gives in, and allows herself to be dominated and exploited by the masculine principle. Instead of questioning this patriarchy as a whole, the Inner Woman subordinates herself to this distorted and one-sided world view. Instead of co-creating a new coexistence of healthy, liberated inner femininity and masculinity, she either submits to the masculine principle (and is inhibited in her power) or tries to climb the ladder of patriarchy herself by adopting the same sick male principles, thereby denying her own femininity. In doing so, she inhibits herself and takes on the role of the toxic Inner Man in order to compensate.

If we carry toxic masculine or feminine sides within us, our relationships are automatically toxic and manipulative and never in line with our true nature. Our relationship becomes a battlefield on which the sick, toxic parts squabble, fight, subjugate, and manipulate each other, according to their own nature.

The solution therefore lies in healing our inner man and our inner woman. To do this, we need to realize the extent to which we ourselves are anchored in patriarchal structures—regardless of whether we are a man or a woman.

# We Are the Creators of Our Reality

The four archetypes described above have another aspect that is important if we want to free ourselves from our old toxic relationships and relationship patterns and install new, nourishing ones: the activity of these archetypes within our psyche ensures that the act of creation is constantly taking place within us. Through the archetypes and their interaction, we create our own reality, whether we realize it or not.

The basic substance of everything is energy and vibration. With our thoughts, feelings, words, and actions or non-actions, we constantly create our very own vibrational pattern. According to the basic Law of Resonance, we attract external vibrations, they resonate with ours, and through this we create our own reality. Whether or not we like our reality, find it pleasant, and are happy depends on the vibrations we carry within us and those we send out. Ultimately, our outside world—and thus, the form and quality of our relationships—functions as a mirror of what's inside us.

The vibrations we send out resonate with the vibrations in the outside world.

We can consciously create our reality by watching over our vibrations, nurturing and constantly optimizing them, and adapting them to the basic vibration of love and our life tasks. Or we can remain unconscious and then have no influence whatsoever on what happens to us and how we react.

## Weakened Inner Man

Jon, 41 years old, divorced, no children, came to the practice because he was "fed up," as he put it, with repeatedly getting involved with women who treated him "like dirt." He had been in three long-term relationships, all of which had followed the same toxic pattern: He met a woman who fascinated him, and since he was intelligent, good-looking, and articulate, had little trouble getting to know her better. The relationship developed quickly but then turned into hell for him, when his partner turned out to be manipulative, selfish, egotistical, and narcissistic.

The more Jon exerted himself and "did everything he could for the woman," the more he slipped into a state of dependency that resulted in him being abused "like a slave" to satisfy the woman's every need. He felt completely dependent. He neglected all other friendships and contacts, and his thoughts only revolved around the woman who tormented, disregarded, and humiliated him.

He had managed to get out of the first two relationships, but the third relationship had lasted longer and now he was married to this woman. Immediately after their marriage, she had manipulated him into giving her the money he had recently inherited. She then threw him out of the house they had shared, which he had signed over to her after the wedding.

During the shamanic work, Jon's Inner Woman appeared sitting on a throne, towering over him. At her feet, lying small and inconspicuous, was his Inner Man. There was no contact between them. The Inner Child lay unconscious behind the throne. The Inner Teacher explained to us that this constellation had come about as a result of Jon's mother. She had suffered greatly from his father's constant escapades, infidelities, and disregard, and repeatedly told Jon that "all men are just worthless, incompetent pigs and don't deserve to be even looked at by a woman." This sentence, which little Jon heard repeatedly, led to the constellation within his psyche that was reflected externally in his relationships.

We began by working on soul retrieval and found a soul contract with the wording "I am worth nothing as a man," which Jon was able to dissolve. After working in various ways for a short time on the soul level, the Inner Man stood up and became taller, the Inner Woman left her throne, and for the first time the two stood facing each other on equal terms with their hands joined. The Inner Child then awoke and joined them, shyly but curiously, watching the change in amazement.

## The Fire of Transformation

The Fire of Transformation is the intrapsychic archetype or place where blocking forces and energies are transformed into inner strength and supportive energy. Here, we can reconnect with lost soul parts and dissolve old soul contracts. Here, we can also meet other beings, archetypes, and souls and resolve unresolved problems and free ourselves from old guilt.

If we are ready, using the power of fire in this place, we can transform everything that burdens us and costs us unnecessary energy and strength or blocks us into helpful, strengthening energies. The Fire of Transformation is therefore the most important intrapsychic place for transforming our toxic relationship patterns. This creates inner freedom and inner strength that were previously bound.

At the same time, the Fire of Transformation is a place of encounter. If something still needs to be clarified on the soul level with other people, whether living or deceased, then that happens in this place. Here, we can work things out, at least on the soul level, with those with whom we are or have been entangled in toxic relationships, who have hurt us, or whom we have hurt.

*The transformative power of fire enables us to transmute negative energies and relationship patterns.*

## Making Peace with Others

If you ask another soul to appear by the Fire of Transformation, it must honour this request. This is a universal and timeless contract to which all souls are bound. The energy of the fire makes it possible to discuss things calmly and ultimately make peace with each other. This is done by forgiving the other soul or asking for forgiveness.

# The Inner Teacher

The Inner Teacher gives us advice and helps when it comes to the important questions in our life. They help us learn and experience actively, consciously, and with joy, and teach us to listen to our inherent wisdom and rely on our intuition. Using their wisdom, the Inner Teacher shows us what we need to do to heal our souls and step out of toxic relationship patterns.

## Learning through and for Life

The Inner Teacher supports us in learning through and for life. The Inner Teacher is closely connected with the wisdom of nature and with upper world teachers who are responsible for our spiritual development and watch over our life plan. The Inner Teacher knows our curriculum and helps and advises us in mastering the individual learning tasks that are necessary to fulfil our life plan in the best possible way. They also help us with specific challenges, such as overcoming our toxic relationship problems.

## Act from Self-Responsibility

The Inner Teacher respects our free will, avoids intervening in our experiences, and does not actively seek contact with us; however, we can get in touch with them and save ourselves many wrong turns and detours and suffering if we follow their advice and wisdom with complete

The Inner Teacher gives us advice when it comes to important questions in our life.

dedication, thereby becoming the creators of our destiny. We also need to reflect on the events in our lives, recognize their meaning and the learning task they contain, then implement the knowledge gained from them.

It is important for us to remain responsible and self-determined, and not relinquish our freedom of choice. We are innovative creators, making our own decisions. We are not beings who passively do what we are told, regardless of the authority from which the instructions may come.

## The Inner Warrior

The Inner Warrior protects our boundaries, ensuring the right balance of closeness and distance. The term "warrior" is not used here to refer to a soldier who fights while holding a weapon. The Inner Warrior corresponds more to the kind of knight or samurai who is completely dedicated to their mission and prepared to give everything for it.

Depending on whether someone is a man or a woman, archetypes such as the Inner Teacher, the Inner Warrior, and the Blacksmith are masculine or feminine.

In our case, this refers to the protection of our inner space, where we feel secure and can unfold and develop in a way that corresponds to our true nature. This, therefore, has to do with the ability to create or maintain a space within ourselves that offers us security, and from which we can consistently overcome internal resistance and obstacles and confidently present our point of view to the outside world.

### Finding and Maintaining Inner and Outer Boundaries

In ancient shamanic tribal cultures that lived in and with nature, there was a fundamental feeling that is unknown to us in our modern world: People felt at one with their fellow human beings, their tribe, surrounding nature, and the cosmos. This feeling of being connected to everything meant that they knew no boundaries in the sense that we perceive them.

In contrast, we often feel separated and isolated. We sense boundaries between ourselves and our environment. Since nobody wants to be isolated, we endeavour to overcome this separation and at least feel connected to something. All too often, boundaries are ruthlessly disregarded and overstepped.

At first glance, people in modern Western society give the impression of being social and treating each other with respect, but behind the scenes, pure selfishness often prevails. Consciously or unconsciously, people are only looking after their own interests. Boundaries are crossed every day, both in the way individuals interact with each other and, on a grander scale, between countries. There's no room for a serving attitude or genuine self-love and altruism in life's daily struggles.

## Healthy Balance between Setting Boundaries and Openness

As a result of their inherent power and strength, the Inner Warrior ensures a healthy balance between setting boundaries and openness and a balance between closeness and distance. They give us the courage to say no wholeheartedly when a person, situation, or task is too much for us or not good for us in some way. They are the guardians and keepers of our personal boundaries.

Too much of this Inner Warrior energy makes us unable to allow any real closeness, causes us to cut ourselves off too much, and leads our soul energy field to be rigid and inflexible. We may also tend to violate the boundaries of others and lack a sense of their personal space.

However, if the energy of our Inner warrior is blocked or weak, our natural ability to set boundaries ceases to function properly. No one then honours the space we are entitled to. We are not taken seriously

| | |
|---|---|
| The Inner Warrior teaches us to stand up for ourselves and not make lazy compromises. | and instead are exploited. No one truly perceives us as we are. Conscious or unconscious fears and insecurities determine our lives. Due to our inability to say no, we constantly overburden ourselves with work that others foist on us. We use up too much of our energy or waste our time with |

pointless discussions and explanations. We are probably surrounded by energy thieves who suck us dry like vampires. In the evening, we are exhausted and lacking in energy.

## Protecting Our Own Space

Only when the power and energy of the Inner Warrior flows freely in our souls can we set our own boundaries outwardly in our normal everyday lives and protect ourselves and feel safe. At the same time, we create a flexible balance between closeness and distance that corresponds to our true nature. The security of our personal space enables us to truly arrive in the here and now and prevents us from looking fearfully into the future and missing out on the happiness of the present moment.

## The Chained Inner Warrior and Loss of Personal Space

Anna, 35, married with a two-year-old child, was toying with the idea of separating from her husband. She explained that she had felt restricted by her husband since the birth of their child. He gave her no space, left her no "air to breathe," causing her to feel increasingly controlled and incapacitated.

She was no longer allowed to meet up with friends, was supposed to be there only for the child and for him, and should preferably just stay at home. During the day, he kept calling her from work to check whether she was at home, and he became increasingly unrestrained and aggressive. She said they had got on very well before the birth of the child, but that she now felt she could no longer set boundaries and that her husband was ruthlessly taking advantage of the fact.

In a shamanic journey, we met her Inner Warrior, who was tied to a tree and could no longer move. Her Inner Teacher came in and explained that a soul part had been lost during the birth of the child—Anna had almost died in childbirth and had had to stay in hospital for a fortnight afterwards. During those traumatic weeks in hospital, Anna had felt powerless when confronted by the doctors and the whole situation, while her husband was severely burdened from having to look after their newborn child on his own.

During this time, and as a result of the loss of soul and the feelings of powerlessness, the Inner Warrior had lost her strength. She could no longer maintain Anna's personal space and, thus, found herself symbolically "tied to the tree." Anna's husband, who had grown up in a toxic family system, had so far done a good job of suppressing the toxic patterns he had inherited from it. However, his feeling of being overwhelmed by the situation activated those patterns, and they filled more and more of Anna's space until she could no longer defend herself against them.

We retrieved the lost part of her soul, freed her Inner Warrior, and re-established fundamental energetic connections. As a result, Anna was well protected once more and able to maintain her personal space. This meant that her husband was thrown back into his own toxic patterns, but fortunately, he realized that he urgently needed help and sought out a therapist with whom he worked through his inner emotional wounds and healed his soul. The young family was then reconciled.

# The Blacksmith

When it comes to relationships, friendships, and connections (of the heart), the Blacksmith is responsible. They show us where we hold onto the past in relationships and don't let go. They dissolve and separate old, outdated connections, cleanse difficult relationships, and free our hearts. They are responsible for everything that holds us back in an unpleasant way, binding our strength and weakening our energy system. They are valuable helpers, especially in toxic relationships.

You may be surprised that the Blacksmith is responsible for connections of the heart. This comes from our Celtic past. Celtic mythology tells us that the blacksmith had a second task in addition to working metal with fire: responsibility for marriages and forging two intertwined rings for the couple.

## Releasing Burdensome Ties

With our Blacksmith, we can dissolve burdensome, outdated attachments and toxic relationships on the soul and heart level, as well as attachments to addictions such as alcohol, cigarettes, computers, sex, food, work, and so on. Anything can become an addiction if it acts as a substitute satisfaction for unlived themes and toxic relationships.

## Encounters Change Us

Every form of encounter and relationship leaves traces within us and our energy system. Even fleeting contacts change our soul energy field for a short time. That is a completely normal process. Even if we don't always realize it, we are constantly communicating with our environment and our fellow human beings—through every thought, every feeling, every word, and every touch. In this way, we weave energetic threads and, depending on the intensity and duration, this can result in a strong relationship that can be either positive, supportive, and enriching or negative, toxic, blocking, and energy-sapping.

> When we meet the Blacksmith, we can clear the energy of strained relationships on the soul level.

The strongest bonds we human beings are capable of are formed through deep love, deep hatred, and deep-seated fear. The more intense our feelings, the stronger and more steadfast the bond becomes. It is wonderful when two people love each other deeply, but who wants to be entangled in toxic relationships?

## A Web of Lines

On the soul level, existing connections show up as relationship lines that lead away from our heart. When we meet the Blacksmith we can see this interweaving of different lines. The different colours show us the status of the relationship in question. Pulsating, mostly red lines correspond to lively, good relationships. The more unpleasant, toxic, and contaminated the connections, the greyer the colour becomes, until it turns black in the case of outlived bonds. Thick lines stand for strong connections, thin lines for weak ones.

# NEGATIVE THOUGHTS, FEELINGS, AND BELIEFS

From time to time, we all have negative thoughts that we neither wish to have nor do us any good. The more we try to simply block these negative thoughts the more we feed them with energy, because we direct our attention towards them.

Thoughts are linked to feelings, even if we are rarely aware of it, and by trying to block negative thoughts, we also feed negative feelings

Thoughts are always linked to feelings. Negative thoughts are associated with negative feelings.

that make our lives difficult and accompany our toxic relationships, such as anger, powerlessness, jealousy, hatred, fear, and so on. Especially those recurring negative feelings that challenge us to explore the thought patterns behind them. This is about consciously recognizing the particular feeling and understanding it as a signpost to our destructive thought patterns.

Many physical reactions are also a direct consequence of our thoughts and feelings. For example, if you think of a lemon and imagine biting into it, you begin to salivate reflexively as a physical reaction; we cannot normally control this at will. Negative thoughts and the negative feelings associated with them also impact our well-being by causing a corresponding reaction to take place in the body via the nervous system, the endocrine system, and many other physiological mechanisms. It is, therefore, important for us to master our thoughts so that we are not at the mercy of them and their consequences.

Typically, it is difficult to simply stop or replace negative thought patterns when it comes to our relationships. We must first heal our soul and deprive negative thought patterns of the fertile ground in which they have germinated and now grow. Ask yourself what damaging, negative thought patterns you find within, when it comes to yourself and your self-worth, and your toxic relationships and the people involved. Think about what you need to change in order to step out of these negative spirals.

## Formative Beliefs

Our thoughts and feelings are often linked to beliefs from our unconscious mind. As we have seen in the model of the different levels of consciousness (see page 38), the subconscious level lies above our soul consciousness. Beliefs are often stored there that keep us stuck in toxic relationships and prevent us from living a fulfilling life and having nourishing, enriching relationships.

Beliefs are our inner attitudes and the guiding principles we believe to be true. We are rarely aware of them, although we often organize our entire lives around them. Beliefs are formed in childhood, when we adopt the beliefs of important caregivers, mainly parents, but also teachers, siblings, or other people who are important to us. Our own experiences also shape our beliefs.

Very intense, traumatic experiences, which are common in some toxic relationships, can also lead to the development of a belief system.

Negative, limiting beliefs can keep us stuck in toxic relationships and relationship patterns and block our exit. In a negative sense, they force us to

Beliefs are generalizations—they generalize and simplify a theme.

do, think, and feel the same things over and over again and chain us to the past, when they were created.

## Examples of Limiting Beliefs

○ I am only loved when I submit.

○ I am worthless.

○ I am not worthy of being loved.

○ I am not allowed to disagree.

○ I deserve to be punished.

○ My opinion counts for nothing.

○ I never manage to stand up for myself.

○ I am not allowed to go my own way.

○ I am responsible for the well-being of others.

○ I am to blame.

There are also supporting beliefs, which we refer to here as affirmations. With their help, we can achieve our wishes and goals.

## Examples of Affirmations

○ I am valuable.

○ I love myself just the way I am.

○ I can do it.

○ I am free.

○ People listen to me.

○ I am free to express my opinion.

○ I am taken seriously, respected, and valued.

○ I have the right to free myself from toxic relationship patterns.

## Healing Old Injuries

Ultimately, all hurtful, negative, and damaging thoughts, feelings, and beliefs have their origin in past events or experiences that have led to a wounding of the soul; therefore, to heal these wounds, it is essential to start at the level of the soul. This is also where we can begin to transform our toxic thought and emotional patterns and negative beliefs using simple means (see page 168).

### Beliefs with a Toxic Effect

Martha, 44 years old, divorced three times, currently single, no children, had a wide range of interests and was well educated. During the initial medical history interview, she explained that she had only ever been attracted to partners who found her fascinating and interesting at the beginning of the relationship and who enjoyed talking to her. Martha loved good conversations and accordingly, she opened up to men who, like her, were well educated and enjoyed in-depth discussions.

With each of her previous husbands, she had been convinced before the marriage that she had found "the right one" this time. As soon as they were married, though, their fascination with her quickly faded and her husbands turned into dogmatists who suddenly no longer wanted to hear her opinions and views.

Martha began to doubt herself. She questioned her views, discounted them, and suddenly started agreeing with her partner's opinions and views "as if inwardly compelled," as she put it, no matter how much they were in conflict with her own. The marriages then increasingly deteriorated into toxic relationships, from which Martha always had to escape. She was unable to explain this pattern of behaviour, especially as she was otherwise skilled at remaining true to her opinions and defending them.

In the shamanic journey, a belief soon emerged with the wording "My opinion counts for nothing." Martha couldn't imagine where this belief had come from, as she couldn't remember it ever having had anything to do with her life. It only came up in her marriages.

Through the shamanic work, we soon learnt that this belief had become firmly established when Martha was about a year old. At that time, her mother had married her father and he had told her mother at every opportunity that her opinion didn't count, only his was right, and she was expected to toe the line. Her father died when Martha was two years old, but as her mother had never spoken about these things, Martha was unaware that these events had influenced her and that the belief had become deeply ingrained.

It was activated in her subconscious each time she married and caused her to repeat her parents' pattern. Once the belief and the connections had been cleared, Martha was able to dissolve this marriage-related belief, by means of a ritual, and free herself from this pattern.

**3**

# WAYS OUT OF TOXIC RELATIONSHIP PATTERNS AND TOXIC RELATIONSHIPS

*If you begin by sacrificing yourself to those you love,
you will end by hating those to whom you have
sacrificed yourself.*

*~ George Bernard Shaw (1856-1950)*

# MAKING A DECISION

Some people remain in toxic relationships because they believe these to be learning experiences that are necessary for them on their spiritual path. This view is fundamentally wrong. We did not come into this world to suffer but to learn and gain experience.

Whether these experiences are painful or joyful is largely determined by our own decisions, beliefs, thoughts, feelings, words, and actions. It can never be our destiny to persevere in distressful, toxic and painful relationships, endure humiliation and allow ourselves to be kicked, nor remain trapped in our own toxic relationship patterns.

The sole learning experience here consists of recognizing that we are stuck in painful soul patterns and then getting up and freeing ourselves from them as quickly as possible. We have the right and even the duty to free ourselves—and through this, our souls—from such relationships and to seek and pursue other paths that bring us joy, fulfil us, and nourish our souls. We are human, and because of our soul purpose, we have the right to activate self-love within us and understand it as the basis of our actions and our relationships.

Only when we feel comfortable with ourselves and treat ourselves lovingly can we set boundaries authentically, say no, stand up for our needs, love others, and treat people lovingly in our encounters and relationships with them. As mentioned in the section on the meaning of life: We can only live a meaningful life and have fulfilling relationships if our whole life is aligned accordingly and

> We are permitted to put ourselves and our well-being first.

if we recognize that the meaning of life has to do with love, laughter, and joy and not strife, rejection, humiliation, hatred, and so on.

If we wish to permanently free ourselves from toxic relationships and relationship patterns and heal our souls, then isolated measures are not enough. Some people believe that they can avoid going through a profound transformation process and that a few new beliefs or simple mental techniques will do the trick. There are many good methods that provide us with momentary and immediately noticeable relief, but they don't solve underlying deep-seated traumas and guide us along a path that will serve us, our lives, and our desire for fulfilling relationships. If we wish to achieve a lasting, permanent change in our relationships, then we are invited to take a path that is certainly painful at times, but which leads us out of our toxic relationship patterns and toxic relationships.

## The Procrastinator in Us

You may back off now and wonder why you would want to go to so much trouble. A voice inside you may speak up and say that it is all not so bad after all. Your toxic relationship is actually easy to put up with. If so, remind yourself once again of why you decided to look into this in the first place: You are suffering, and you have the right and, from the soul's point of view, the obligation to free yourself from your situation and find new ways of relating that enrich and nourish you and give you joy. Now and again, we all tend to give up in certain areas of life and not even start to face our problems. So it is up to you. It is now time to make clear decisions:

o Are you ready to make a real change in your life, in your toxic relationship structures and toxic relationship patterns, instead of carrying on as before?

○ Are you ready to leave your comfort zone?

○ Are you ready to take full responsibility for yourself, your relationships, and your life?

○ Are you ready for your truth?

If you can answer with a clear "Yes," all these questions, then you are ready to set off on the journey to the land of your soul. Do not let your doubts, fears, or reservations slow you down.

As soon as we start thinking about leaving our familiar stamping ground, the procrastinator and the boycotter in us will try to prevent us from exploring the positive aspects these new paths would bring. They try to convince us that these paths are far too dangerous and will inevitably kill us. The risk is far too high. Of course, the risk is far too high—not for us and our souls, but for the boycotter and procrastinator in us, because the more we walk our path in clarity, the more they will have to surrender their supremacy.

Good preparation and planning enable us to take calculated risks. There is indeed a risk that we will not achieve the desired or hoped-for outcome, but doing is part of learning and being alive. If we never muster the courage to try something new, we remain trapped in the same old hamster wheel.

Life is synonymous with change.

Children still have this natural curiosity about life. If they were afraid to take the first step, they would never learn to walk. If they didn't get up again after falling down, they would not develop any further.

Growth is only possible if we change old, outdated structures, or even leave them behind, and break new ground.

Unfortunately, as we develop, we unlearn and forget this natural curiosity within us and, instead, give more and more room to fear and lethargy. We are afraid of failure and doubt our own strength and creative power, so we suppress the basic principle of life, change, and prefer to stagnate.

Let's now summon up our courage and open ourselves to the possibility that we can decide to free ourselves from all toxic relationships, heal our souls, and build nourishing, enriching, and happy relationships.

## Solutions for Our Toxic Relationship Problems

You can now decide which path of liberation you wish to take. I am assuming that you are serious about it and have no wish to remain in your toxic relationships or toxic relationship patterns. There are three options open to you, each with different consequences.

The first step is the same in all three options: You end the relationship or relationships that you perceive as toxic. For example, by quitting your job, ending your partnership, saying goodbye to supposed friendships, or breaking off contact with those members of your family with whom you have toxic relationships, such as parents, siblings, grandparents, and so on, at least temporarily.

> Persisting in toxic relationships is not a solution.

This, of course, requires courage and the willingness to accept the consequences. Avoiding this step is not an option, unless your partner or the other person is prepared to undergo therapy and work on themself and with you in depth.

### The Bogus Solution

You end your toxic relationships but take no further action to enable yourself to experience and live fulfilling relationships in the future. Then, according to the Mirror Law and the basic Law of Resonance (see page 69), it is virtually inevitable that you will continue to experience toxic relationships in your life.

## The Small-Scale Solution

You end your toxic relationships and heal the most fundamental causes in your soul that have led you into such relationships until now. You can find out how to do that in the following chapters of this book.

## The Large-Scale Solution

You end your toxic relationships, heal the causes in your soul, recognize your purpose, and follow the call of your heart and soul in all areas of your life. In doing so, you go far beyond simply creating a healthy, nurturing relationship and set out to utilize your own creative power and purpose for the benefit of all beings. You are on your way home. To do this, you can embark on your own personal hero's journey, which we will discuss briefly on pages 170–173.

# HEALING THE SOUL
# IN DIALOGUE WITH THE SOUL

So, what can we do to free ourselves, heal our souls, and transform our toxic relationships and relationship patterns?

The shamanic healing path described below is one way in which you can proceed. Whether you wish to, or need to, take all the individual steps will depend on your personal history, your current personality structure, and your soul wounds. Just look openly and honestly at which themes resonate with you and which path would be right for you.

This is how you can create your path out of toxic relationship patterns and toxic relationships:

○ Start with an honest assessment.

○ Take preparatory and supporting measures:

– Create a ritual framework in a protected space.

– Burn incense for support and guidance, and bring in the power of the Devas (the plant souls whose powers are released when you burn incense).

– Open the sacred space, thereby activating supporting forces.

– Form a simple protective circle for your work.

○ Create a clear vision of how you imagine good, fulfilling, loving, nurturing relationships, friendships, work relationships, or contacts within your family to be.

○ Clear and strengthen your aura and chakras.

○ Harmonize the energy of the four elements. Activate the power and support of your ancestors, and heal any blocking forces in your family of origin that contribute to toxic relationships.

○ Get in touch with your soul via the Shamanic Soul Journey, Light.

– The Journeys to the Fire of Transformation; to the Inner Teacher; to the Inner Warrior; to the Inner Blacksmith; to the Inner Man, the Inner Woman, and the Inner Child.

– The Journeys to Retrieve Lost Soul Parts; to Reclaim Potentials; to Dissolve Soul Contracts; to Dissolve Beliefs.

○ Don't give up too soon. Keep going until you have reached your goal.

○ If you want to take the path of freedom and healing even further, create your own hero's journey.

Through taking these steps, you can heal your soul and transform blocking forces within your psyche, thereby creating different conditions so that you no longer bring toxic relationships into your life.

## Get Support If You Need It

Please note: You can probably carry out most of these solution steps yourself with no problem. As discussed in the model of the levels of consciousness (see page 38), blocking phenomena that keep you stuck in toxic relationship patterns can also occur on other levels. You may like to continue with shamanic work in order to delve deeper into the wisdom of your soul. It would then make sense to ask a suitably trained therapist for support or learn the shamanic journeying technique in appropriate courses.

> The path of self-healing the soul creates the conditions for happy relationships.

If you get stuck at some point or other, find yourself therapeutic shamanic support and guidance. It is not a sign of weakness but a sign of strength to recognize your limits, admit them, and find help.

# An Honest Assessment

Being honest with yourself about your situation is the basis for change. However, various mechanisms prevent us from recognizing our toxic relationships are a problem and freeing ourselves from them. These reaction patterns, which are described below, apply in principle to everything we want to change, even if we are not yet ready to do so, have not recognized the problem, or want to avoid change.

## Ignoring, Denying, and Suppressing

We don't want to admit to ourselves that we have a problem and are stuck in a toxic relationship. We pretend everything is fine and try to suppress the truth. If this suppression is successful, we shift the associated negative feelings and toxic energies into our subconscious. But this has neither freed us from them nor solved anything.

## Fighting

In order to overcome them, we try to fight our problems and negative, blocking, and disease-causing patterns, thoughts, and feelings. However, this tactic can never work, because where our energy goes, our entire inner system always follows. This means that the more energy we put into the fight, the more we feed the problem we want to get rid of.

In this way, it becomes increasingly well fed and has no reason to leave.

If we only fight this battle internally the toxic relationship remains, along with our feelings of suffering, pain, guilt, powerless anger, and so forth, which may even increase. If we also fight the battle externally, we argue with our opposite number in this toxic relationship or use toxic behaviour patterns ourselves. The toxic relationship may then blow up in our faces but our inner toxic relationship patterns don't change, and we soon slide into the next unhealthy relationship structure.

## Negotiation

In negotiation, we don't lash out wildly to defeat our troublesome internal companions but engage in an inner dialogue to persuade our problem—our toxic relationship and the feelings associated with it—to leave us alone, using arguments, enticements, concessions, and reason.

Unfortunately, this tactic has limited success, because as with fighting, our attention is directed towards the problem not its solution. If we engage in negotiations with a toxic partner without having healed our inner emotional deficits and problems, this usually results in us becoming even more entangled—our partner tormenting us further through manipulation and us doubting ourselves even more.

## Falling into Depressive Moods

We have given up and are dominated by feelings of not being able to change anything. We have failed in all our efforts to suppress, fight, and negotiate, and we no longer believe in change.

If we get stuck in this phase, we feel helpless, incapable of acting, frozen, sad, and paralysed with fear. We leave the field completely open to the manipulating, degrading, and humiliating behaviour on the part of our toxic counterpart.

We are all individual, so we all deal with our problems and toxic relationship patterns differently. Perhaps you already know which of the mechanisms described above is your inner boycotter's favourite pattern—the one they use again and again to prevent you from making the necessary changes. If so, write down what comes to mind and the consequences this has for you, your wishes, and goals. Also think about what you can and must change in order to free yourself from it.

## Freeing Yourself from the Chains of Toxic Relationships

How can we free ourselves permanently and avoid repeating old patterns? The shamanic path offers solutions to this problem, some of which we will look at. First, though, it is important to recognize the reaction patterns, described above, that are not working and replace them with acceptance and letting go.

> Avoidance strategies will not get us one step further.

### Acknowledging and Accepting

At this point, we are ready to acknowledge our problems and negative thoughts and feelings and accept that they are there and we are trapped in toxic relationships and relationship patterns. We symbolically embrace the problem as an "energetic being," in that we respect and honour it, begin to listen to it—and therefore to ourselves, and take our suffering seriously. Absolute honesty is required at this point, so that we don't deceive ourselves.

### Letting Go

In the first step, we have acknowledged our problem, our negative thoughts and feelings, our pain and suffering, and so on, and we have accepted that we are stuck in toxic relationships and relationship patterns. We can now embark on an honest, profound path of self-healing and heal our soul. We can finally let go and free ourselves. This works

100 percent of the time, as long as there is no longer a resonance field within us and we are truly at peace with ourselves.

## The First Step towards Self-Healing

Now take a piece of paper and a pen. The best thing to do is to create a calm, meditative setting; for example, by lighting a candle, playing meditation music in the background, and burning a blend of incense you like. Make sure you are not going to be disturbed for a while and can concentrate fully on yourself.

Take a few deep breaths, connect with your heart, listen to yourself, and then write down, in the form of a letter, what tactics you usually use to push away the truth about your toxic relationship and associated suffering from your life. Write down how you honestly feel. Don't think too much when writing; just write down everything that comes to mind about your situation.

In this way, you recognize your current situation and, at the same time, through writing, create inner distance. You take everything inside and place it in the outside world, so you can hold it in your hands in the form of the letter. This is the first step towards self-healing and freeing yourself from your toxic relationship structures.

In the letter, name the person with whom you are in a toxic relationship and describe how you react to this person. Here is an example of what your letter to yourself could look like:

Dear (your name),

Whenever my toxic boss humiliates me, I just put up with it. Instead of standing up for myself, I simply ignore his insults and pretend that nothing has happened. It makes me feel guilty, small, and inferior.

# THE RITUAL FRAMEWORK

If you want something to change, you need to take the time and create adequate space to clarify for yourself, using your inner wisdom, what is really important to you and what you really want. This is necessary in order to scrutinize your relationships and relationship patterns and make honest decisions without being influenced by others. Only then can you embark on a path of self-healing.

Make sure that you are undisturbed when working on your toxic relationship patterns. It is helpful to set fixed times to do this. Think about when would be best for you, and where and how you can create a protected space in which you can be undisturbed and open yourself up to your inner wisdom.

It is important not to be influenced by any toxic partner you may still have.

Shamanic work requires a simple, ritual framework. Light a candle, burn incense that you like or one of the recommended incense substances, perhaps play meditation music, and have a shamanic drum rhythm in the background so that you can make contact with your soul and embark on your healing journey through the light trance this induces.

Take yourself seriously. Agree on fixed times with yourself, when you can work undisturbed on your themes.

## The Shamanic Drum Rhythm

In order to enter the land of the soul, activate self-healing, and free ourselves from toxic relationship patterns, we need to enter the shamanic state of consciousness through a light trance. This can be achieved by using a specific drum rhythm. Our brain is very receptive to certain rhythms and vibrations, as can be observed in an EEG. Drumming increases the proportion of alpha waves and theta waves, which are present in half-sleep or trance states. The deep relaxation required for this is impressively demonstrated in the measurement of brain waves. You will find a shamanic drum sequence for free download on: **https://schamanenpfad.de.**

> In shamanism, the monotonous, constant rhythm of a drum has always been important for entering shamanic levels of consciousness.

## The Incense Ritual for Support

Incense plays a central role in shamanism. With incense, we create a ritual framework and accompany and support the shamanic work. Our sense of smell gives us direct access to our limbic system, meaning that we bypass the filter of our rational brain and go straight to the area responsible for our emotions.

When we burn incense, we connect with the soul energies of the incense substances, known as devas, which unfold their helping, healing, and supportive influence through the smoke and the fragrance. It is important to use incense or blends that support you in your endeavour. Various incense blends specially created for shamanic work are recommended for our shamanic path of soul healing that help us to free ourselves from toxic relationship structures. Fire and embers enable us to form our own connection to these incense plants.

## What Does Burning Incense Do?

The material plant components are converted into smoke by the fire, transferring the essence of the plants to the subtle level. Through the mucous membranes of the nose, the active ingredients released by the plants reach the limbic system, the oldest part of our brain in terms of phylogeny, which is responsible for processing emotions and instincts and which controls many vital functions such as our stress behaviour and hormonal balance. The fragrances released by burning incense have a stimulating, relaxing, healing, clarifying, invigorating, and purifying effect on body, mind, and soul.

## Please Note Carefully

You should follow a few basic rules to ensure that burning incense has no unpleasant side effects:

○ Temporarily switch off any smoke detector installed in the room where you are burning incense, and don't forget to reactivate it after burning the incense and subsequent airing of the room.

○ Depending on how much incense you put on the embers, you will produce more or less smoke. Be aware of yourself and your sense of well-being. The effect is not dependent on the smoke production, but on the intention and clarity with which you perform the incense ritual. Burning incense should never make you feel uncomfortable.

○ If you are prone to allergies, burn incense with caution and check the ingredients.

○ After completing your incense burning ritual, air the room thoroughly, carefully dispose of the glowing charcoal (fire hazard!), and reactivate the smoke alarms.

## Basic Blends for Incense Rituals

The following four incense blends form the basis for many incense rituals in all kinds of shamanic work. Their energy and effect are ideally suited to freeing us from our toxic relationships and relationship patterns and healing our soul. You can make the blends yourself or order them from our shop : www.schamanentraum.de. You can also use other incense blends with similar effects.

## Incense Blend for Purification

This Purifying blend consists of frankincense, sage, copal, and thyme. These are the effects of the ingredients in the blend:

o **Frankincense** has a strong purifying effect. It supports our inner soul powers.

o **Sage** purifies and clears the aura, neutralizes disruptive energies, and creates space for new energy. It is said to have a germicidal effect.

o **Copal** harmonizes our body, mind, and soul; relaxes and calms us; pulls us out of emotional lows, and connects us with courage and drive.

o **Thyme** strengthens our resistance on all levels, has a disinfectant effect and supports us in courageously going our own way.

> The Soul Message of the Purification Blend
> Liberate yourself and your surroundings
> from any burdensome energies,
> and free your light-filled being once again.

## Incense Blend for Protection

This Protecting blend consists of juniper berries, copal, cedarwood, and lavender flowers. These are the effects of the ingredients in the blend:

○ **Juniper berries** provide strong protection against dark, negative, and disruptive energies. They help you recognize your own limits, enabling you to set your boundaries more effectively.

○ **Copal** harmonizes our body, mind, and soul; relaxes and calms us; pulls us out of emotional lows, and connects us with courage and drive.

○ **Cedarwood** restores our self-confidence and strengthens our soul.

○ **Lavender flowers** protect against negative influences.

> **The Soul Message of the Protection Blend**
> Create a protected space
> in which you can unfold freely
> according to your soul's intention.

## Incense Blend for Centring

This Centring blend consists of frankincense, myrrh, peppermint, and verbena. These are the effects of the ingredients in the blend:

○ **Frankincense** clears and centres our mind. It promotes alertness and clarity.

○ **Myrrh** promotes concentration and has a calming effect. It helps ground us.

- **Peppermint** sharpens and calms the human mind.

- **Verbena** promotes clarity and centring of the mind.

> ## The Soul Message of the Centring Blend
> Leave all the ifs and buts behind,
> and stand by yourself and your values
> in a centred and clear way.

## Incense Blend for Blessing

The Blessing blend consists of frankincense from Eritrea, Benzoin Sumatra incense, and coloured frankincense. These are the effects of the ingredients:

- **Frankincense** makes us receptive to higher vibrations, strengthens our intuition and vision, and connects us with the divine.

- **Benzoin** is said to be purifying, uplifting, and stimulating. It melts away blockages, clears negative energy, and promotes generosity.

> ## The Soul Message of the Blessing Blend
> In connection with divine wisdom,
> follow your path for the benefit of all beings.

We establish a connection to the incense blends and their energy by burning them during a ritual. In shamanic work, the energies that are released support us with their power, wisdom, and love, and through the main effect and the soul message of the particular blend. This means we have powerful helper energies at hand that support our path out of toxic relationships and accompany us on the path to soul healing.

The "Incense Ritual to Strengthen and Clear the Aura" is described on page 143. You can also use these instructions as a basis for other incense rituals. There are, of course, a whole host of other incense rituals. If you enjoy incense, you can also create your own incense rituals or enrich your life with different incense substances and blends.

If you have never burnt incense before, you can find instructions and further information on **https://schamanenpfad.de.**

# THE SACRED SPACE AND
# THE PROTECTIVE CIRCLE

Healing and change always take place in a realm of reality that lies beyond our normal space–time structure. This "sacred space" is like a bubble that is connected to spatial and temporal infinity.

The sacred space is of such importance because only here can we reach the energy field of the soul. At the same time, it prevents any difficult situations, memories, traumas, and stressful situations being brought into the here and now.

At the beginning of each ritual, you open the sacred space and create a protective circle.

## Opening the Sacred Space

To open the sacred space, take time to carefully read the following text:

○ I turn my attention and my breath downwards and ask the healing powers of Mother Earth, which heal the feminine pole, to connect with me and with my energy field. [Establish the connection by taking a few deep breaths.]

○ I turn my attention and my breath upwards and ask the healing powers of Father Sun, which heal the masculine pole, to connect with me and with my energy field. [Establish the connection by taking a few deep breaths.]

○ I turn my attention and my breath to the South and ask the healing powers of the South, which heal the wounds of the past, to connect with me and with my energy field. [Establish the connection by taking a few deep breaths.]

○ I turn my attention and my breath to the West and ask the healing powers of the West, which heal fear of the future and of death, to connect with me and with my energy field. [Establish the connection by taking a few deep breaths.]

○ I turn my attention and my breath to the North and ask the healing powers of the North, which heal all blockages in family systems, and in the systems of families of origin and the ancestors, to connect with me and with my energy field. [Establish the connection by taking a few deep breaths.]

○ I turn my attention and my breath to the East and ask the healing powers of the East, which lead to clarity of vision and my life task, to connect with me and with my energy field. [Establish the connection by taking a few deep breaths.]

○ I now turn my attention, supported by my breath, inwards to my heart centre and imagine a cross whose four axes are formed by the four elements: fire, earth, water, and air. [Establish the connection by taking a few deep breaths.]

○ I turn my attention and my breath to the space behind me, to the element of fire and ask the healing powers of fire to connect with me and my heart. [Establish the connection by taking a few deep breaths.]

○ I turn my attention and my breath to the space in front of me, to the element of earth and ask the healing powers of earth to connect with me and my heart. [Establish the connection by taking a few deep breaths.]

o I turn my attention and my breath to the left, to the element of water, and ask the healing powers of water to connect with me and my heart. [Establish the connection by taking a few deep breaths.]

o I turn my attention and my breath to the right, to the element of air, and ask the healing powers of air to connect with me and my heart. [Establish the connection by taking a few deep breaths.]

o I am now in my centre, in my sacred space, and I ask all those healing powers and spiritual forces that wish to support my ritual for their help and protection.

When you open the sacred space, make sure that you are fully focused. You activate the space through your intention, your imagination, and your breathing in order to establish contact with your soul.

## The Protective Circle

In order to remain undisturbed and uninfluenced and allow yourself to establish contact with your soul and heal it, you need a spiritual protective circle. To build it, ask the stinging nettle, one of the great shamanic protective plants, for its support.

If you have ever, by accident, touched a stinging nettle, you probably jumped back involuntarily. Contact can cause severe skin irritation, redness, and sometimes painful itching. On the soul level, the nettle has the same effect, but only if a foreign form of energy approaches that would disturb or harm us.

The stinging nettle deva, the soul energy of the plant, prevents foreign energies from penetrating our sacred space through its energetic reaction to such contact, thereby establishing a protected space for us. This gives you a

> To create a protective circle, we connect with the stinging nettle deva, with the supportive and protective soul energy of the stinging nettle.

powerful accompanying soul energy, which enables you to work undisturbed. Proceed as follows:

○ Picture a stinging nettle in your mind's eye.

○ Inwardly ask the soul energy of the plant to create a protective circle around you. For example, say: "I ask the stinging nettle for support and protection in my soul healing."

○ Then imagine being enveloped and protected by the stinging nettle deva.

## Protection in Everyday Life

The protective circle is, of course, not only helpful for shamanic work. You can also create it at any time in your everyday life, in any situation in which you need protection—when encountering people who display toxic behaviour, for example.

# ACTIVATING SELF-LOVE

Many people have lost touch with themselves to such an extent that they no longer have any awareness of themselves and their needs and no longer sense or know what is really good for them. They no longer have any connection to self-love. This connection is essential if we want to free ourselves from toxic relationships and relationship patterns and heal our soul in order to find a path to freedom.

We don't have to earn self-love (or love); it is simply there. So it is not about working on self-love, but about re-establishing and activating the connections that open up our contact with self-love.

We can do this in a ritual, first establishing the connection between our three centres of wisdom: Head, abdomen, and heart. This is the precondition for going on a shamanic journey into the chamber of self-love, in a further step, in order to activate our connection to self-love there.

## Ritual: Connecting Head, Abdomen, and Heart

**Preparation**

Give yourself 30 minutes when you will be undisturbed, and create a calm, relaxed atmosphere. Light a candle and, if you like, burn an incense blend of your choice or the centring blend. Open the sacred space, and create a protective circle with the nettle deva (see pages 131–134). Play a shamanic drum rhythm or meditation music in the background.

## Procedure

- Focus your attention on your breathing, and breathe deeply, in and out. Notice how your chest rises and falls in rhythm with your breath and how the air flows through your nose and throat into your lungs. Allow yourself to sink deeper into the ground with each exhalation and feel how you are carried by Mother Earth.
- Images from your everyday life may pop up in your mind. Don't hold onto them; let them pass like clouds in the sky.
- Now turn your attention inwards to your heart. Start by breathing there, feeling into this region of your body and simply observing your heart as it beats steadily and pumps blood through your body.
- Realize that your heart is also the place that connects you to your ability to love, to your ability to love yourself, to altruism, and to the unconditional love that created this universe.
- Remain in your heart for a while using your attention and breathing.
- Now move your attention and your breath from your heart upwards into your head, to your brain.
- With each breath, create a circuit that connects your head brain and your heart brain.
- When you breathe in, you draw the power of love from your heart into your head, and when you breathe out, take the energy of your thoughts and feelings, which are located in both halves of your brain, down to your heart. This creates a cycle that connects your heart with your head.
- Now move your attention and your breath from your heart downwards to the region of your upper abdomen, to your solar plexus, above your navel.
- This is the home of your intuition.
- With each breath, create a circuit that connects your heart brain and your abdomen brain.

- As you breathe out, allow the power of love to sink from your heart into your abdomen, and as you breathe in, take the energy of your intuition and inner wisdom, which is located in this area, up to your heart. This creates a cycle that connects your heart with your abdomen.
- Expand this energy flow and breathe from your abdomen via your heart into your head and back down again. This is how you create a balance between these centres within you.

**Conclusion**
Keep your attention on this cycle for a while. Then take a deep breath, thank yourself, and end the ritual.

# The Shamanic Journey into the Chamber of Self-Love

Through this ritual you have reconnected your head, abdomen, and heart. Your inner wisdom centres are no longer working in isolation but, ideally, in harmony with one another. From this connection, you can also begin exploring yourself, your past relationships, and your idea of your future nourishing relationships in a new and holistic way, going within to find out what it is you truly want.

Then go on the shamanic journey into the chamber of self-love. Love for ourselves is stored there as an infinite source, and our only task is to re-activate our connection to it. You can download the text for *The Journey into the Chamber of Self-Love* from **https://schamanenpfad.de.**

# CREATING A CLEAR VISION

Do you have a clear image of good, fulfilling, loving, nourishing relationships, friendships, work relationships, and contacts within your family?

Unless this is the case, you will be unable to replace your toxic relationships with nourishing ones, because you will be sending confused messages to the universe. After all, how can the universe support you and send you the right people and opportunities if you don't know what you truly want? So, visualize your image of your relationships and what it is you want.

The clearer you are internally, the closer your entire system can align itself with your goal. So make sure you take the time to create a vision of how you imagine your future relationships will be, once you have released them from toxicity, healed your soul, and are inwardly free.

**You need a clear vision to enable your system to align with it.**

The following ritual will help you develop your vision of your future nourishing relationships. Then perform the ritual "Like a Tree" in order to connect your ideas and visions with the supporting energies of Father Sun and Mother Earth and give them the strength to be realized. After that, read the letter you wrote while working through the section called "The First Step towards Self-Healing" (see page 123). Having done this, write a second letter to yourself in which you write down your vision and your goal.

# Ritual: The Vision of the Heart

The following ritual can help you find out how you imagine your future relationships will be and what your heart truly desires. To do this, go on a little vision quest into your heart. Listen to it, and recognize your true heart purpose with regard to your ability to relate to others.

## Preparation

Give yourself 20 minutes in which you will be undisturbed, and create a calm, relaxed atmosphere. Light a candle and, if you like, burn an incense blend of your choice.

Open the sacred space and create a protective circle with the nettle deva (see pages 131–134). Play a shamanic drum rhythm or meditation music in the background.

## Procedure

- Close your eyes and breathe deeply, in and out. Observe the rhythm of your breath without consciously influencing it. Allow everything to be that is there right now—all the thoughts, feelings, and sensations you have. But don't hold onto them; stay with your breathing.
- Now turn your attention inwards to your heart. Start by breathing there, feeling your heart, and observing how it beats constantly and pumps the blood throughout your body.
- Realize that your heart is also the place that connects you to your ability to love, to your ability to love yourself, altruism, and the unconditional love that created this universe.
- Remain in your heart for a while using your attention and breathing.

- Now listen within yourself, and ask for a picture, an idea, a sense, or a hint of what it is you desire, from the bottom of your heart, for your relationships; what your heart's intention is; what your personal vision is, and how you wish to feel in your relationships in the future.
- Images may appear, you may hear a sentence or see a word in front of you, and your feelings may simply change, enabling you to sense how you would like to feel in the future. Stay with it for a while, until a feeling of peace and clarity sets in.

**Conclusion**

Take a deep breath and thank yourself, your heart, your intuition, and your inner wisdom, then end the ritual.

## Ritual: Like a Tree

The best insights won't help you if you fail to draw any conclusions from them, if you fail to initiate any processes of change, if you fail to act. The ritual "Like a Tree" helps you connect your ideas and the visions of your future nourishing relationships with the earth and the sun and give them the power to be realized.

We connect the new state we wish for to our heart, the energy of the sun, and the energy of the earth, so that it can grow and flourish powerfully, and ultimately manifest here in this world. The aim is not to get stuck in the spiritual principle, in the idea, but to actively connect with your own earthly creative power and the energy of your heart in order to actively bring about change.

## Preparation

Give yourself 30 minutes when you will be undisturbed, and create a calm, relaxed atmosphere. Light a candle and, if you like, burn an incense blend of your choice. Open the sacred space, and create a protective circle with the nettle deva (see pages 131–134). Play a shamanic drum rhythm or meditation music in the background.

## Procedure

- Start by focusing your attention on your breathing, and breathe deeply, in and out. Notice how your chest rises and falls in rhythm with your breath and how the air flows through your nose and throat and into your lungs.
- Images from your everyday life may pop up in your mind. Don't hold onto them; let them pass like clouds in the sky.
- Now think about how you would like to organize your relationships in the future and how you would like to live them in reality in your everyday life. Imagine your vision, your goal, expanding in your heart and filling it completely.
- Now turn your attention downwards, to the soles of your feet. With each exhalation, be more in touch with the ground beneath your feet, and feel the way in which you are being carried by Mother Earth. Imagine that roots are growing downwards from the soles of your feet into the earth, connecting you ever more deeply and firmly with Mother Earth. Then imagine as you breathe in that you are absorbing the grounding, connecting, and materializing power of the earth through your roots, and direct this energy to your heart.
- Observe how, in your heart, the energy of your vision of your future relationships connects with the energy of the earth. Now slowly move your attention upwards, to the highest point of your head. From there, imagine yourself connecting with the energy of the sun like the canopy of a tree, and imagine this energy flowing down from the sun

and into you through streams of energy. Then imagine as you breathe in that you are absorbing the grounding, connecting, and materializing power of the earth through your roots, and direct this energy to your heart.

- Observe the energy of your vision of future nourishing relationships connecting with the energy of the sun and the energy of the earth in your heart. Then, together with your breath, send this energy out into the world with every exhalation. Do this until you feel you have established a secure, stable connection, feel relaxed, and peace returns.

## Conclusion

To finish, take a deep breath. Thank yourself, your inner wisdom, and the wisdom of Mother Earth and Father Sun, and end your ritual.

# A Letter to Yourself

Write a second letter to yourself in which you change all the statements about your toxic relationship structures you wrote down in the first letter (see page 123) and wanted to heal, into statements that are as positive as possible and feel good to you. You formulate the letter as a goal; that is, where you want to go. Use the present tense and the "is" form; for example: "My relationship with my father is relaxed, and I'm recognized and loved just as I am," not "I would like . . ." For your soul and your subconscious, this has much more power than formulations using "would be," "could be," and "should be."

# STRENGTHENING AND CLEARING THE AURA

## Ritual: Incense for Strengthening and Clearing the Aura

The incense ritual to strengthen and clear the aura has the following aim:

- To release negative energies stored through toxic relationships.
- To cleanse your aura of blocking patterns that negatively affect your ability to relate to others.
- To protect your aura so that toxic relationship energies are no longer stored and you are able to set your own boundaries more easily.
- To realign and recentre your aura so that it corresponds to you and your true nature.
- To "bless" your aura, to connect it to the divine, enabling you to be much better connected to supporting forces and your own inner wisdom.

For the incense ritual, you will need the four incense blends already described – purifying, protecting, centring, and blessing (see pages 127–130) or comparable incense blends or incense substances with the same effect.

## Preparation

Switch off any smoke detectors. Give yourself half an hour in which you will be undisturbed, and create a calm, relaxed atmosphere.

Have your incense and a candle at hand and make sure you have a fireproof surface. Light the charcoal and allow the embers to develop. Light the candle.

Open the Sacred Space and create a protective circle with the nettle deva (see pages 131–134). Play a shamanic drum rhythm or meditation music in the background.

## Procedure

- Place the **purifying incense blend** on the glowing charcoal and wait briefly until it releases its fragrance and smoke.
- Place the incense burner on the floor on a fireproof surface.
- Stand over the incense burner with your legs slightly open.
- As you stand in the smoke of the incense and inhale, imagine that you are absorbing the purifying qualities, and that all blocking, negative energies in your entire energy field are being released. Your energy field is being cleansed.
- As you exhale, in your imagination breathe all the released negative energies into the smoke and through your legs into the earth and ask Mother Earth and the energy of the purifying blend to transform and dissolve the energies for the well-being of all. When you inhale, you reconnect with the purifying effect.
- Repeat the process several times.
- Now remove the remains of the incense mixture from the charcoal and replace it with the **protecting incense blend**.
- Stand over the incense burner once more, with your legs slightly open.
- As you stand in the smoke of the incense and inhale, imagine that you are absorbing the protecting qualities, and that the protecting effect is spreading throughout your entire energy field.

- As you exhale, let your breath flow downwards towards the incense, and as you inhale, reconnect with the protecting effect.
- Repeat the process several times.
- Now remove the remains of the incense blend from the charcoal and replace it with the **centring incense blend**.
- Stand over the incense burner once more, with your legs slightly open.
- As you stand in the smoke of the incense and inhale, imagine that you are absorbing the centring qualities, and that the centring effect is spreading throughout your entire energy field.
- As you exhale, let your breath flow downwards towards the incense, and as you inhale, reconnect with the centring effect.
- Repeat the process several times.
- Now remove the remains of the incense blend from the charcoal and replace it with the **blessing incense blend**.
- Stand over the incense burner once more, with your legs slightly open.
- As you stand in the smoke of the incense and inhale, imagine that you are absorbing the blessing qualities, and that the blessing effect is spreading throughout your entire energy field.
- As you exhale, let your breath flow downwards towards the incense, and as you inhale, reconnect with the blessing effect.
- Repeat the process several times.

### Conclusion

Finally, thank all those energies and beings involved for their support and help, and also thank yourself for your drive and for carrying out the incense ritual.

Carefully dispose of the glowing charcoal and the remains of the incense blends (caution: fire hazard) in the toilet, for example. Extinguish the candle and leave the incense burner to cool in a safe place. Then air the room thoroughly and reactivate the smoke alarms.

You can perform the incense ritual as often as required.

## Incense Ritual as an Aura Cure

As our aura is directly and immediately affected by any negative energies and toxic behaviour around us, it is advisable to perform this incense ritual every day for at least a week or even several weeks. This also releases older and stubborn negative energies and blocking patterns. In addition, you can use other incense blends that match your current themes (Self-Love, Transformation, The Lovers, and on).

# HARMONIZING THE CHAKRAS
# AND THE FRONTAL EMINENCES

Each chakra fulfils different energetic tasks at any given time and rotates either clockwise or anti-clockwise, depending on what is needed, and with varying intensity. The entire system is optimally coordinated, as all energy centres communicate with each other in a permanent exchange of information. This harmonious overall balance is important for the distribution of energy in the soul energy field and the nervous system.

As noted earlier, a simple but highly effective method of de-stressing and relaxing the chakras, as well as harmonizing and balancing the energies, is to work with the frontal eminences, or anti-stress points. These two points can be used for relaxation and stress reduction on all levels.

The points are located in two small depressions on lines that run from the centre of each eyebrow upwards, to approximately halfway between the eyebrows and the hairline. You can use them whenever

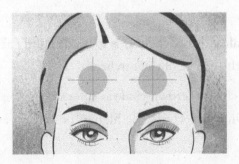

Fig. 3: The Frontal Eminences

you are stressed in everyday life and after spending time with people with whom you are stuck in a toxic relationship. You can perform this de-stressing ritual as often as you like.

## The Position of the Chakras

In order to use this ritual for de-stressing, you need to know the location of the chakras. To recap: the first chakra has an energy funnel pointing vertically downwards and the seventh chakra has an energy funnel pointing vertically upwards. Chakras 2 to 6 have horizontal energy funnels, both to the front and to the back. Since it is difficult to reach the funnels on the back of your body, in the following ritual simply imagine them being harmonized by directing your attention there.

o The first chakra (root chakra) is located at the end of the coccyx between the sexual organs and the anus.

o The second chakra (sacral chakra) is located two to four finger widths below the navel.

o The third chakra (navel chakra) is located just above the navel and below the sternum, in the area of the solar plexus.

o The fourth chakra (heart chakra) is located centrally at the level of the heart.

o The fifth chakra (throat chakra) is located at the level of the larynx.

o The sixth chakra (brow chakra) is located slightly above the eyebrows in the centre of the forehead.

o The seventh chakra (crown chakra) is located at the crown on top of the head; in other words, the highest point of the head.

Fig. 4: The Chakras

## Ritual: Harmonizing the Chakras and the Frontal Eminences

### Preparation

Give yourself 30 minutes when you will be undisturbed, and create a calm, relaxed atmosphere.

Open the sacred space, and create a protective circle with the nettle deva (see pages 131–134). Play a shamanic drum rhythm or meditation music in the background.

### Procedure

- We always start with the first chakra and then move upwards, step by step, to the seventh chakra.
- Stand up straight in a relaxed position, and ask your inner wisdom for guidance. Concentrate on your feet, and imagine that deep roots are growing down into the earth from the soles of your feet.

149

- Gently touch the anti-stress points on your forehead described on page 147 using two fingers of one hand. This signals that you now want to de-stress and harmonize with your body's system.
- Now move your attention to the first chakra. Shape your other hand into a cup and hold it about 20 centimetres in front of the funnel of the chakra. This shows your body's system where the de-stressing should take place. This happens of its own accord; our will plays no part, and we leave the work to our inner wisdom.
- Now breathe consciously into the chakra, and ask for this chakra to be harmonized and de-stressed. In addition, imagine that, as you exhale, everything that inhibits, blocks, or weakens this centre or holds it in a state of excessive energy and excitement is being discharged into the earth through the soles of your feet.
- Keep doing this until you notice a change in your hand; for example, a tingling sensation, a pulsation, or a change in temperature. This signals that the stress has been released.
- Now move your attention and your hand to the second chakra, then to the third, and so on, up to the sixth chakra in front of your body, and finally to the crown chakra, then repeat the process.
- After that, direct your attention to the chakras on the back of your body in the same way. If you cannot reach them with your hand, simply imagine that you are holding your hand in a cup shape at the corresponding point.
- It is important to be fully present with your attention and imagine that the chakra in question is being harmonized, strengthened, and balanced.

**Conclusion**
When you have reached the crown chakra, moving up your back in this manner, end the ritual. Sense how you feel for a while longer.

# HARMONIZING THE ENERGY OF THE FOUR ELEMENTS

## Ritual: Harmonizing the Energy of the Four Elements

As long as the energy of one or more elements is completely or partially blocked, we are in an energetic imbalance. This has an impact on our relationships, which reflect the theme of the blocked or weakened element, and this in turn favours toxic relationship patterns. This means we need to remove blockages and weaknesses. This can be done by performing a constellation ritual with the four elements to check and restore the energy flow.

For the following ritual you will need five stones—for example, large pebbles—and five pieces of paper and a pen.

**Preparation**
Before you start the ritual, remind yourself of your goal and what it is you wish for: You want to free and heal the energy of the four elements within you from blockages and toxic elements so that they have a positive effect on your relationships, enabling you to free yourself from all toxic relationships and toxic relationship patterns and heal your soul.

Make sure you are going to be undisturbed for the next 30 minutes, and create your ritual framework. Open the sacred space; ask the nettle deva for protection (see page 131–134).

Play a shamanic drum rhythm or meditation music in the background.

Burn the Purifying blend of incense, and hold all the stones you will be using for the ritual in the smoke. Then place the stones on the floor as shown in the illustration.

Write the name of each element (fire, earth, water, or air) on one of four separate pieces of paper, and write "My Heart – The Centre" on the fifth piece.

Place the leaves next to or under the stones as shown in the illustration.

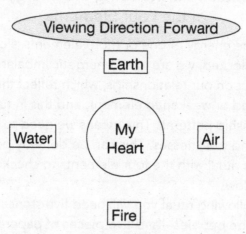

Fig. 5: Harmonizing the Four Elements

## Procedure

Start by standing over the stone that represents the position of the heart. Your gaze is directed forward.

Breathe deeply, in and out. Be conscious that, in this constellation, you are now freeing the four elements within you from any blocking energies so that their power is available to you and your relationships, in harmony with, and according to, your nature.

Connect inwardly with the self-love within you, and imagine that this power is filling your heart.

Then move to the stone that stands for the air element, stand over the stone, and perform the following sequence:

- Connect to this position and the energy of its element, and to the self-love that you have just activated within you.
- Imagine that, when you breathe out, the healing power of love flows to the soles of your feet, and when you breathe in, it flows back into your heart, dissolving any blockages, fears, and feelings of guilt.
- Do this until you feel that the full, pure power of the element is flowing again without obstruction.
- Thank the energy of the element, and go to the stone representative of the fire element.
- Repeat the process there, and move on to the stone representative of the water element. Repeat the steps there, move on to the stone representative of the earth element, and repeat the process once more.
- Finally, go back to the centre, to the position of your heart, and stand there. Feel into yourself and the four elements once again. If you still feel a lack of harmony, repeat the whole process.

## Conclusion

Thank your elements and your heart for their support and end the ritual. Thank the stones for their help, and purify them by either burning the purifying blend of incense and holding them in the smoke, placing them in the sun, or holding them under running water.

# ACTIVATING THE POWER
# OF THE ANCESTORS

Through our origins, we are integrated into the force field of our ancestral line. Everything that has happened in the last seven generations influences us and our lives, and also our ability to relate and our relationships themselves. If there are blockages in this area, we need to clear them so that we have enough available energy and there is nothing that slows us down or holds us back. If it is free of blockages, the ancestral force field strengthens us. The wisdom of these ancient men and women accompanies us through our lives and has a supportive effect on our relationship skills. The following constellation ritual will help you to optimize the necessary energy flow.

> We do not repeat the unhealed toxic relationship patterns of our ancestors.

## Ritual: The 7-Generation Constellation

For the following ritual you will need nine stones; for example, large pebbles, and nine sheets of paper and a pen.

**Preparation**
Before you start the ritual, remind yourself of your goal and what it is you wish for: You want to free yourself from all toxic relationships and toxic relationship patterns and heal your soul.

Give yourself 30 minutes when you will be undisturbed. Open the sacred space, and create a protective circle with the nettle deva (see pages 131–134). Play a shamanic drum rhythm or meditation music in the background.

Burn the Purifying blend of incense, and hold all the stones you will be using for the ritual in the smoke. Then place all the stones in a row on the floor.

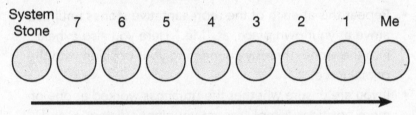

Fig. 6: The 7–Generation Constellation

Write the numbers 1 to 7 on seven separate sheets of paper, and write "System" and "Me" on the two remaining sheets of paper. Place the sheets of paper next to or under the stones as shown in the illustration.

**Procedure**

- To begin with, stand over the "System" stone, and inwardly ask your ancestors for their support, healing power, strength, and love. Engage in an inner dialogue with them. Explain to them that, through the primal force, the wisdom, and the love stored in the system, you now want to dissolve any blocking energies that are stored in the energy field of your ancestors that are keeping you stuck in your toxic relationship patterns, so that the pure primal force can again flow freely for everyone. Take your time to have a loving dialogue with your ancestors.
- Then breathe deeply, in and out, a few times, and imagine with each inhalation that you are taking in the healing primal force stored in the system and that you will carry it in your heart from now on.

- Then take a step forward, and stand over the stone representative of the seventh generation.
- Breathe deeply, in and out, a few times, and with each exhalation imagine that the healing power is helping release any issues that may be impeding your path to happy, fulfilling, and nourishing relationships.
- Then go to the stone representative of the sixth generation, and repeat the process.
- Repeat this at each of the representative stones until you arrive at your own place, at "Me." Here you also exhale into the stone, thereby connecting your position with the primal force.
- If you are unsure whether the ritual has worked at one or more positions, simply repeat your inner dialogue, and continue to use the breathing technique described until you feel the impulse to move on to the next stone.

**Conclusion**

At the end of your ritual, thank your ancestors for their support. Thank the stones for their help, and purify them by either burning the purifying blend of incense and holding them in the smoke, or placing them in the sun, or holding them under running water.

# THE SHAMANIC SOUL
# JOURNEY, LIGHT

For our shamanic path of soul healing, and to free ourselves from toxic relationship structures, we use a simple variant of the classic shamanic soul journey. Anything else would go far beyond the scope of this book. It is also advisable to learn the shamanic travelling technique under guidance in appropriate courses.

With the simple travelling technique presented here, you can meet different archetypes in your soul garden and activate them to help you achieve your goal. You can retrieve lost soul parts and potentials and dissolve old, blocking soul contracts and beliefs.

**Please note:** In everything that has to do with retrieving soul parts and potentials as well as the dissolution of soul contracts, it is vital not to force things by using your mind and ego. Follow the instructions exactly. This is where we are closest to the emotions of our deepest traumas; therefore, don't try to open up things in your soul that are not yet ready to heal or that require the help of a shaman experienced in soul retrieval. Respect your own limits, accept with gratitude what is possible now, and don't rush things. The following journeys all follow the same pattern.

Be aware of your limits, and stick to the instructions. It doesn't all have to happen at once; you can repeat the journeys at any time.

## Ritual: Shamanic Soul Journey, Light

### Preparation

Start by defining the exact goal of the journey you want to take, which should always be in the context of the vision that you formulated in the The Vision of the Heart ritual (page 139). For example, if you are travelling to your Inner Warrior, then formulate this as clearly as possible for yourself: "I am travelling to my inner warrior to clarify the extent of my current ability to set boundaries and find out what I can do to optimize it in a way that corresponds to my true being."

Then create a ritual in a relaxed setting, in a protected, distraction-free room, by burning incense and lighting a candle. Open the sacred space, and ask the nettle deva for protection (see pages 131–134).

### Procedure

With the support of the shamanic drum rhythm, these instructions will now accompany you during your transition from normal waking consciousness to soul consciousness. You set off on your journey:

- You first meet the guardian of your soul garden (or your power animal, if you are a shamanic traveller).
- With the guardian, you make your way to the Fire of Transformation, where whatever you came here to do takes place.
- At the Fire of Transformation, you meet the intrapsychic archetypes that can help you resolve your toxic relationship patterns; here at the fire, lost soul parts also return and you dissolve soul contracts and beliefs.
- After spending a few minutes by the Fire of Transformation, you return from soul consciousness to normal waking consciousness.

### Conclusion

Finally, write down the information you have received during your shamanic journey. If there is something you need to do in your everyday life, do it.

You will find the instruction text for this journey at the end of the book (see page 181), so you can create your own audio file to be able to journey through the stages more easily.

An accompanying shamanic drum rhythm is important to help you enter a light trance. A variety of mp3s or CDs with appropriate drum sequences is available. You can also download an audio file with a suitable drum rhythm from our website at **https://schamanenpfad.de**.

## The Journey to the Fire of Transformation

In the Shamanic Soul Journey, Light you always travel to the Fire of Transformation. There, you can ask for a specific archetype to appear or address a different concern. Read this section before you embark on your journey to the Fire of Transformation.

You will find the Fire of Transformation deep in your soul garden. The guardian of your soul garden will guide you there in the Shamanic Soul Journey.

When you arrive at the fire, the way in which it can work in you at that moment is indicated by its appearance.

### The Strong Fire

If the fire burns steadily, evenly, and vibrantly, with a mostly bluish-violet flame, then it is in its full power and can perfectly fulfil the transformation work. In this form, it is also a wonderful place to meet and create peace.

## The Overpowering Fire

If the fire is so overpoweringly hot that it is impossible to stay near it, then this is an indication that the principle of transformation has taken on a life of its own and the balance in the process of taking, holding, giving, and letting go has been disturbed.

It can also be an indication that we are refusing the process of transformation and cannot or do not want to forgive ourselves or others. In this case, all attempts to free ourselves from our own toxic relationship patterns are initially more difficult or even impossible until the fire burns more favourably. By summoning your Inner Teacher (see page 161) and engaging in a dialogue with them and the "essence of fire," we can clarify why this is so and what we can do to reduce the fire to its natural strength.

## The Weak Fire

If the fire is weak and fails to burn properly, this is a sign that our ability or willingness to transform ourselves inwardly and in reality is weakened. Here, too, it is important to summon the Inner Teacher and clarify in a dialogue with them and the "essence of fire" why this is so and what we can do to restore the fire to its natural strength.

## The Extinguished Fire

If the fire has been extinguished, we are incapable of any real transformation, and we are probably also unable to really forgive anyone. Here, too, it is important to summon the Inner Teacher and clarify in a dialogue with them and the "essence of fire" why this is so and what we can do to rekindle the fire. A soul part may be trapped in an old trauma.

## Ensuring a Healthy Fire

If you realize during the journey that your fire is not burning properly, then you have already found a significant reason for why you have not yet been able to transform your toxic relationship patterns. Ask your Inner Teacher to appear at the fire (see the following journey), and ask them and "the being of fire" itself what you can or must do to enable your fire to burn again with the strength that is right for you. After the journey, start implementing this in your life.

> ### Transformation in the Fire
> If your fire is burning optimally, stretch out your hands towards it, and imagine that everything that has been keeping you stuck in toxic relationship patterns and preventing healing is now flowing into the fire through your hands and being transformed into a field of support and strength.

# The Journey to the Inner Teacher

When you journey to your Inner Teacher, think carefully about what you need from them. Ask them to appear at the Fire of Transformation. Treat them with respect, and ask for advice and help. The Inner Teacher usually appears in the form of a person, but can also appear as an animal or mythical creature.

Even if you are not specifically journeying to your Inner Teacher, for some journeys it is important to invite them to come to the Fire of Transformation.

In rare cases, your Inner Teacher may appear weakened or ill and not provide any information. This means that your innate learning system is either not working at the moment or is weakened. In that case, ask your Guardian and your Inner Teacher for specific information on what you need to do to reactivate your inner learning system.

## When Your Inner Teacher Appears Spontaneously

Inner Teachers often appear spontaneously at the Fire of Transformation during a journey. If your Inner Teacher considers it important to appear, listen carefully to what they have to say. Thank them for their advice, and implement it consistently in your everyday life.

# The Journey to the Inner Warrior

During a shamanic journey to our Inner Warrior, we see the current state of our ability to set boundaries reflected in their state of being. Our Inner Warrior reflects our ability to face the adversities of life and the toxic patterns in our relationships in an appropriate way. So pay attention to their state of being when you meet them at the Fire of Transformation.

## If Your Inner Warrior Is Too Weak

If your Inner Warrior is injured, chained, or unarmed, ask your Inner Teacher to explain to you which people, relationships, and life circumstances are draining your energy. Ask them for precise instructions on what to do. On your journey, you may need to symbolically loosen the chains.

Ask for an explanation of the cause of the weakness. Such weaknesses are often old injuries from childhood in connection with beliefs. Let them explain to you how you can heal them. If other people are involved in causing the weakness, make peace with them internally. In this way, you can reinvigorate your Inner Warrior, step by step.

## When Your Inner Warrior Is Too Strong

If your Inner Warrior is extensively armed, rigid, or immovable, there is probably a part of you that has been hurt in the past and is, therefore, afraid of encounters and relationships that nourish you and give you joy. Talk to your Inner Warrior to clarify the causes. How did this lack of flexibility come about?

## Recommendation for Everyday Life

Be playful when it comes to your personal boundaries, and in your relationships and encounters with people, check how much physical distance you really need to feel comfortable. This signals to both the Inner Warrior who is too strong and the Inner Warrior who is too weak that you are now consciously addressing these issues in your everyday life.

The boundaries we set in order to protect ourselves in our different encounters and life situations are unique to us as individuals. One person may need more distance in relationships, another may need less. The radius of this area around you depends on a variety of changing factors, such as how you feel on the day, your degree of health and mental alertness, and the people you are dealing with. Once you have explored your personal radius in your relationships, check whether other people respect it or repeatedly violate it. Visualize your Inner Warrior patrolling this border and not letting anyone get closer than is good for you.

# The Journey to the Inner Blacksmith

When you meet your Inner Blacksmith at the Fire of Transformation, explain why you have come. Your Inner Blacksmith will not normally talk much but will start work immediately, and the various relationship lines they are working with will become visible.

## The Inner Blacksmith Who Goes about His Work

If the relationship lines are black and have outlived their time, they can be severed, because they burden our hearts unnecessarily. The Inner Blacksmith will sever these lines with a sword. If the relationship lines

The Inner Blacksmith severs or cleanses your relationship lines, thereby dissolving toxic patterns.

are contaminated in places, and therefore discoloured, the Inner Blacksmith will remove the deposits with a knife or scalpel so that they are free of contamination once more. After completing his work, he may give you tasks for your everyday reality.

## The Inner Blacksmith Who Refuses to Do His Work

If the Inner Blacksmith appears and does nothing, ask for an explanation of this inaction. You may still have to forgive someone inwardly or ask someone for forgiveness before the relationship lines can be severed. Parent–child relationship lines and lines between a husband and a wife who have a child together can be purified but not severed.

## Recommendation for Everyday Life

Pay particular attention to your feelings in your relationships and everyday encounters in the near future, not just the toxic ones. Take your time, and honestly consider how you feel about them.

For example, is the behaviour of your colleague or partner annoying you and draining your energy? Or does this behaviour make it difficult for you to achieve your goal or realize your wish or dream? Do you still react to a friend in a reserved and distant manner because of an old argument, and does this rob you of vital energy or distract you?

The point here is not to end these relationships, but to recognize which aspects are burdening you and your relationships with the people concerned so that you can become sensitive to this unnecessary heaviness. In all these cases, you can perform the purifying ritual described later, which will enable you to meet people in freedom once more and no longer be distracted.

# The Journey to the Inner Man, the Inner Woman, and the Inner Child

The journey to the Inner Man, Inner Woman, and Inner Child archetypes is about recognizing how they interact with each other, whether there is a balance between the Inner Man and the Inner Woman, whether they can merge into the archetype of The Lovers, and how your Inner child feels about this.

Travel to the Fire of Transformation, and ask your Inner Woman, your Inner Man, and your Inner Child to appear. After a short time, they will appear at the fire. Observe whether they come to the fire together or individually, whether they treat each other lovingly and courteously, or whether husband and wife are obviously out of balance. See if they turn away from each other or if one is maybe tormenting the other, oppressing them, not taking them seriously, and so on. Observe the Inner Child as well. Look closely at how they behave and feel.

Ask them to tell you how they are. Ask whether your Inner Woman and Inner Man can merge into the archetype of The Lovers. Ask what they all need in order to find their strength and vigour. Just listen to what they have to tell you. Try not to judge, assess, or evaluate, but stay with them with your full, undivided attention.

# The Journey to Retrieve Lost Soul Parts

The aim is to reintegrate into our soul system those soul parts that have separated off in the past, are ready to return, and are important for healing our toxic relationship patterns. With the Shamanic Soul Journey, Light, however, we can only retrieve soul parts that have already regained their original power, wisdom, and strength and no longer carry the original soul injury. Still traumatized and injured parts require deeper treatment and should only be retrieved by an experienced shaman.

When you arrive at the Fire of Transformation, start by connecting with the energy of this place and ask your Inner Teacher to appear. After they have sat down with you, ask inwardly for all those soul parts that have regained their power, strength, and wisdom and are ready to return to the wholeness of your soul, to appear at the fire.

If soul parts then appear, ask them if they would like to tell you something of their story, and listen to them. Also ask your Inner Teacher if they have a message for you concerning what you can or must do in your life to allow the parts that are now returning to feel safe, secure, and comfortable with you.

If no soul parts appear by the fire during the journey, ask your Inner Teacher whether any soul parts are missing that could be retrieved with this Shamanic Soul Journey.

In your imagination, take the soul parts by the hand, and walk with them directly through the fire. There, the parts that were previously separated merge with your soul, and their energy is once more available.

## Integrating the Retrieved Soul Parts

Realize that the reunification of soul parts will require integration work. Give yourself a few minutes every day for the next four weeks to do this. Regardless of whether you can feel the energy of the soul parts or not, take yourself symbolically in your arms and greet the soul part(s) so that they feel welcome and can heal your soul. The soul parts may otherwise depart again if they feel unappreciated, disregarded, and unloved.

You should not make the journey to retrieve soul parts too often, because this might be demanding too much of yourself. It is better to concern yourself with their integration into everyday life. Only travel back to the fire when you feel completely at one and the soul part has been fully integrated.

## The Journey to Retrieve Potentials

A potential, similar to a soul part, is a missing part of your soul. The difference is that a potential always comprises an ability that you lost in a previous incarnation due to traumatic experiences. This can, for example, be the ability to love deeply, be happy, talk to others, stand up for your point of view, and so on.

The journey and the integration work is exactly the same as in the journey to retrieve soul parts, except that, at the Fire of Transformation, you ask for the corresponding potentials to return to you.

## The Journey to Dissolve Soul Contracts

Your Inner Teacher will also support you on your journey to dissolve soul contracts. When you have reached the Fire of Transformation, ask your Inner Teacher to appear. Ask them if there are any soul contracts that bind you to the person or people with whom you are trapped in toxic relationships, or if you have made a soul contract with yourself that keeps you stuck in your toxic relationship patterns.

If your Inner Teacher says yes, then ask your Guardian to retrieve the soul contract (or soul contracts) from the Cave of Soul Contracts—for example, in the form of a document—and bring it to the fire. Your Guardian will disappear and reappear a short time later with the document. Read it through carefully, and ask your Inner Teacher if they have anything else to say. When you are ready, commit the document to the flames of the Fire of Transformation with the request that the soul contract be dissolved and transformed in the flames. Watch the document burn.

### Transformation of Soul Contracts in Your Reality

After your journey, write down the content of the soul contract (or soul contracts) exactly. Realize how much it has influenced your relationships so far. Write down everything you can think of without giving it too much thought. Then burn the note or bury it in the ground. Be aware that, through this ritual, you will finally release yourself from the binding power of the soul contract and be free of it.

# The Journey to Dissolve Beliefs

You go through the same procedure for the journey to dissolve beliefs as for the dissolution of soul contracts. You travel to the Fire of Transformation and ask your Inner Teacher to appear. Ask them if there are any beliefs that are preventing you from stepping out of your toxic relationship patterns and healing your soul.

If your Inner Teacher says yes, then ask your Guardian to retrieve the belief (or beliefs) from the level of the subconscious—for example, in the form of a document—and bring it to the fire. Your Guardian will disappear and reappear a short time later with the document. Read it carefully, ask your teacher if there is anything else they want to tell you, and when you are ready, commit the document to the flames of the Fire of Transformation, and ask that the beliefs be dissolved and transformed in the flames. Watch the document burn.

> Negative beliefs lose their power when, in the Fire of Transformation and ritual, we transform them in reality.

## Transformation of Negative Beliefs in Reality

When you return from your journey, you perform another ritual. Write down the belief (or beliefs) in detail. Realize how much they have influenced your relationships so far, and write down everything that comes to mind. Don't think about it too much. You can then burn the note in reality (note the fire hazard) or bury it in the ground. Be mindful, and realize that through this ritual you are finally releasing yourself from the binding power of the belief. You are now free of it.

# Support through Affirmations

If you like, you can continue working with affirmations (see page 108) after each journey, especially after dissolving beliefs and soul contracts. Find a suitable affirmation that reinforces your inner freedom and supports you on your path to happy relationships.

Write the affirmation on several pieces of paper, and hang them in different places in your home so that you are continually reminded of it. Make a habit of imagining that you are breathing in the affirmation with your breath. Do this over several days or weeks, until you feel that the energy and power of your affirmation is being realized in you, in your reality, and in your relationships.

---

### Stick to Your New Path
### and Don't Give Up Too Soon

On our journey through life, there will always be points at which we would prefer to give up. We feel unable to manage, and we question everything. Especially at such points, it is important to remind yourself of your goal, to remain consistent and not give up too soon. Your journey is only over when you have reached your destination.

Only when you have ended the old toxic relationship patterns and healed your soul, only when you have created new relationship structures that nourish you, support you, and bring you joy, will you have reached your goal.

So, if you do get to the point where you have doubts, visualize your goal again and again and do the rituals "Like a Tree" (see page 140) and "Connecting Head, Abdomen, and Heart" (see page 135).

---

# YOUR PERSONAL HERO'S JOURNEY

In order to heal toxic relationship patterns, toxic relationships, and the resulting injuries to our soul and walk a path that brings us closer to our purpose at the same time, we can follow the shamanic path of the Hero's Journey. In doing so, we embark on a journey that takes us far beyond the relationship level and can also lead to the large-scale solution (see page 117).

We encounter many different variations of the Hero's Journey in mythology and heroic stories. The basic theme is always as follows: The protagonist is either prompted or forced by life in the form of an inner call or external events, such as strokes of fate or other challenges, to leave their normal everyday life. They set off on a journey to achieve a specific goal (kill the dragon, save the princess, find the Holy Grail, and so on). The Hero's destination is far away from their previous home environment and initially seems almost out of reach. On their journey, our Hero encounters all kinds of challenges, tasks, and dangers that life throws at him. They have to master them all and grows continuously in the process. Finally, they have acquired all the skills they need to face themself in the darkness, to confront their longings, their desires, their fears and deepest truths, and so on, and to master themself.

On their journey, the hero grows, becomes stronger, and is finally transformed.

Now our sublimated Hero is strong enough. They know who they are and the true reason for their being on this journey. They continue on the path to healing and finally reach their destination. There, they

170

are once again tested by life and have to prove that their intentions are serious. They must prove themself worthy of having their deepest desires fulfilled as a gift. If they clear this final hurdle as well, their purpose will be fulfilled. They have reached the end of their journey and return home transformed. They stay there until they feel the call once more and set off on their journey to continue growing and mastering their life.

In our case, the call is to free ourselves from the sickening and degrading patterns of toxic relationships so that we can steer our lives, or certain areas of our lives (partnerships, family, work relationships, friendships), in a direction that promotes our joyfulness, our contentment, and our health once again.

If you would like to embark on your own Hero's Journey, you will find references to relevant literature and an online course in the Resources section.

## The Soul Wheel

Our Hero's Journey, which we undertake in order to heal our toxic relationship structures and underlying soul wounds and soul issues, leads us through the Soul Wheel. The Soul Wheel symbolizes different areas of life, which we will look at more closely and work on during the course of the journey, so that we can heal our soul and bring it into harmony.

The Soul Wheel as depicted on page 173 symbolizes 12 steps that are necessary to move from "toxic relationships" to "nourishing, happy relationships" and heal our soul in the process:

1. **Assessment:** We start our journey by assessing our current situation and determining our destination.
2. **Self-love:** We open up to loving ourselves, this being the most important prerequisite for a successful journey.

3. **Head, heart, and abdominal brain:** We connect the three most important centres of wisdom within us: Head brain, heart brain, and abdominal brain. In this way, we create the necessary conditions to ensure that we don't proceed with blinkers on and overlook important aspects, but instead take a holistic approach to healing.

4. **Activating the fields of power:** We activate our three most important sources of strength within our psyche: the Source of Life, the Place of Strength, and the Rock of the Ancestors. This gives us the energy we need to free ourselves from the chains of toxic relationships and relationship patterns.

5. **Releasing the chains of the past:** We release the chains of the past, heal old wounds, and transform the patterns that are blocking us into a field of power.

6. **Overcoming fears of the future:** We transform our fears of the future into a field of courage, confidence, and joy.

7. **Activating creative power in the here and now:** We activate our own creative power in the here and now, so that we can shape our lives and relationships the way we would like them to be.

8. **Recognizing your vision and purpose:** We embark on a vision quest to recognize our life vision and our life task.

9. **Activating your inner healing power:** We connect with our own inner healing power, and activate it, so that healing can take place on all levels.

10. **Healing the energy field:** We heal our energy field, our aura, and our chakras, so that they can work perfectly again. This ensures that we no longer emit or attract energies that would lead to toxic patterns.

11. **Healing cell memory:** We heal our cell memory, so that it is free of any blocking patterns. It then promotes and supports our health once more and no longer contains patterns that would keep leading us into toxic relationships. We erase all those memories and patterns at the cellular level that are stored there due to our toxic experiences and patterns and those of our ancestors.

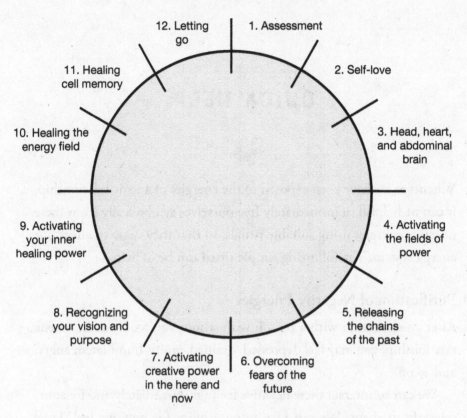

Fig. 7: The Twelve Areas of the Soul Wheel

12. **Letting go:** We let go of everything that is still holding us back, blocking us, and keeping us in a negative, toxic relationship cycle. We then pass through the gateway to our destination. Our soul is free, and we have freed ourselves from all those energies that have kept us trapped in toxic patterns.

# QUICK HELP

Whenever we have been exposed to the energies of a toxic relationship, it can be helpful to immediately free ourselves symbolically from these negative energies using suitable rituals, so that they cease to affect our energy system. The following simple ritual can be of help.

## Purification of Negative Energies

After an encounter with a person with whom you are stuck in a toxic relationship, you may feel depressed, drained, guilty, humiliated, angry, and so on.

We can counteract these negative feelings immediately and free ourselves from them. We can take responsibility for how we feel, leave the role of victim behind, and step into our creative power. Instead of blaming the other person for our feelings, instead of allowing toxic feelings to rage, thereby disempowering ourselves, we can work proactively and increase our ability to remain calm and take care of ourselves.

## Ritual: Purification of Negative Energies

The following ritual will help you free yourself from any negative emotions and energies you have taken on as a result of the encounter. It takes 10–20 minutes, and you will need a shower.

## Preparation

The ritual takes place in the bathroom. Create a meditative setting by playing a shamanic drum rhythm or meditation music and lighting a candle. If you like, you can also burn the Purifying blend of incense. Open the sacred space, and create a protective circle with the nettle deva (see pages 131–134).

Now pay close attention to how you are right now and the feelings you are experiencing. Realize once again that no one has power over your feelings except you. You are the creator of your reality and you take responsibility for how you feel.

## Procedure

- Turn on the shower and select a water temperature that is comfortable for you. Stand naked in the stream of water.
- Once again, notice your current feelings and then imagine them being washed away from you with the water and disappearing down the drain. Ask the transformative power of the water to transform all the negative energies flowing away from you so that they are harmless and can no longer hurt anyone.
- You can enhance the effect of this ritual through your breathing. As you inhale, imagine that the air you breathe is connecting with the energy of the negative feelings that lie deep down. As you exhale, imagine that, with the air you breathe, these negative feelings are being channelled directly into the stream of water and are flowing away. Keep doing this until you feel better and a sense of inner peace sets in.

## Conclusion

After the ritual, thank the water for its support, dry yourself thoroughly, and then purify yourself with the protecting, centring, and blessing incense blends, as described in the "Incense Ritual for Strengthening and Clearing the Aura" (see page 143).

# Protection from Negative Energies

If you know that an encounter will be accompanied by negative toxic emotions and energies, you can protect yourself beforehand, or during the situation as it arises. There are different methods for doing this:

○ You have already learnt about the **protective circle with the stinging nettle** (see page 133). You can work with it mentally before or during any toxic relationship situation.

○ An excellent option is to burn **incense**. For energetic protection from the negative energies of the toxic relationship, you can, for example, burn incense with a Protecting blend before the encounter. To do this, stand over your incense burner on the floor, as described in the "Incense Ritual for Strengthening and Clearing the Aura" (see page 143). As the smoke of the Protecting blend flows around your body, you connect inwardly with your intention to be better protected and visualize how the incense stabilizes your aura, creating a protected and safe space around you.

○ Another excellent option is to **work with our Inner Warrior**. As already described (see page 100), the Inner Warrior is the archetype within the psyche that provides a protected, safe space for us, where we can feel comfortable and develop according to our true being. Simply close your eyes and breathe deeply, in and out, several times, and imagine a warrior whose task is not to wage war but to protect your personal space. Ask them inwardly to ensure that you are safe and protected on a soul level and that negative energies from the outside cannot harm you.

# FINALLY – WHAT IS REAL LOVE?

Finally, let us remind ourselves once again of how our whole life consists of a multitude of relationships. We build relationships during the time of pregnancy, long before our birth—with our mother, with our father, and, of course, with the environment in which our mother moves and lives her life.

As soon as we see the light of day, we enter into a relationship with the visible world in which we live. During our childhood, we expand our experience of the space around us further, and enter into new relationships with people, animals, our growing environment, and, of course, ourselves. We experience ourselves in the context of our inner life in relation to the outside world. And so it goes on and on.

We are expanding our awareness of the nature of the world, and all of this happens through our relationships. Relationships determine our whole life. It is, therefore, worth taking a closer look at the relationship structures and patterns we have stored in our soul and subconscious, and healing everything that poisons, restricts, disrupts, and hinders our relationships and fundamentally prevents us from being happy.

We can take a big step towards fulfilling relationships, and consequently to a fulfilled life, through healing our soul and working with the appropriate techniques, as described in this book. However, our relationships will not change simply because we read this book or look into other healing methods.

Only through doing and acting can we change the corresponding structures in a material world.

This is life's invitation to us all: By shaping our lives, by taking action, by moving forward, and at the same time opening our consciousness more and more to our true self—love—we steadily unveil once again the joyful being with happy, fulfilling relationships we always have been, always are, and always will be.

Let us, therefore, take another look at love. It should be clear by now that toxic relationships prevent love and have nothing to do with love. Love can only be experienced and lived when we have freed ourselves from all toxic relationship patterns and healed our souls—when we are inwardly truly free.

In the section on the meaning of life, we mentioned love as one of life's goals. But what exactly do we mean by that? Love cannot be understood rationally; it can only be experienced. Most people describe love as an emotion or a feeling. From a spiritual perspective, however, love goes far beyond this. Love is the basic principle of creation and this universe. It is the building material from which everything is made. It is the subtle energy from which this universe is woven.

We often confuse our feelings and emotions with love, although they simply arise from love. Most emotions, however, arise when we are not in a state of love. Love leads to inner freedom and expansiveness, to a merging and dissolving of the "I." It is not something you can really give or receive, because love in its true form is simply there, unlimited, infinite. It is available to all beings because it is the basic substance of everything. WE ARE LOVE!

If our awareness of this were omnipresent, and if we were able to grasp the full extent of it, then we would be capable of immediate and boundless love. There is nothing that is not made of love, even if, in the form of a shadow, it may often appear to us to be distorted and evil.

This is no longer about the love between two or more people, or about the separating and dividing love that is of our own making, but about the energy behind everything. It is about unconditional, all-encompassing, non-judgemental divine love, such as Jesus gave to us in Christian culture: "Love your neighbour as yourself. Love your enemies."

This has nothing to do with weakness or cowardice, but with true inner greatness, courage, and the ability to love unconditionally. The whole of life, with all its positive and negative aspects, is constantly challenging us to step out of evaluation, to not judge and condemn but step into love. Every encounter, including and especially with ourselves, every friendship and every loving relationship, is a training ground for recognizing this basic principle and re-establishing it as the basis for our actions.

Human, enhancing love is a breath of divine love and can remind us of where we really come from and what love is. This human form is linked to emotions and feelings, which can often be negative and painful. Some claim that the more you suffer, the greater your love. But suffering has nothing at all to do with love.

Genuine love sets you free and has no wish to possess. As long as we want to possess something—an object, a place, an animal, or a person—we are not in a state of love. This thinking always arises from the wounded parts in us that are continually screaming, "I want this, I need that . . ." Our ego wants and wants. Genuine love, on the other hand, knows that ultimately it is impossible to possess anything at all, that every form of possession makes us unfree. Real love exists in a state of free consciousness; it lets go and knows that it is impossible to possess anything. Love is devotion to something higher, including our higher self. Love gives up all attachment and surrenders to the universe and to life.

Human love always moves into differentiation immediately. It can only arise because we live in a polarized world. Here we have love and its opposite pole, hate. We have happy and unhappy relationships, dependency and freedom, and so on. There are always two poles of any basic principle reflected in this field of tension. Both poles are labelled with a judgement, rejection, or approval. As soon as we find ourselves in this field of tension of rejection or agreement, we have left freedom and true love, and the drama of life in which we are trapped arises. We may or may not like something, that is human and part of our lives, but it has nothing to do with love. It has to do with attachment to something that has not been resolved. Comprehensive, universal love reveals itself when we relinquish human, clinging love and transform it into something greater.

Now it is up to you to make your own life decisions. Will you decide in favour of:

○ yourself and your happiness or yourself and against (self-)love?

○ authentic, nourishing and enriching encounters and relationships or further toxic relationships?

○ the courage to walk your path and heal yourself and your soul or lingering in fear and diseased structures?

○ love or against it?

○ a path that leads you to yourself, or against it?

I wish you all the best on your journey. May love always be your guide. May you find and walk your path to healing your soul. And may you free yourself from all burdensome toxic relationships.

—**Stefan Limmer**

# APPENDIX

## TRANSCRIPT OF THE
## SHAMANIC SOUL JOURNEY, LIGHT

---

**NOTE**

On page 158/159 you will find an overview of the steps of the journey. Please note the information, and carry out your preparations. Make sure you will be undisturbed for the next 30 minutes. If you wish to, light a candle and burn the Purifying or Protecting incense blends or another incense you find pleasant. Play the shamanic drum rhythm, open the sacred space, and ask for protection from the nettle deva (see pages 131–134).

What you should do at the *Fire of Transformation* to enable you to take the steps towards self-healing is described in the individual chapters from page 159 onwards.

---

Welcome to this shamanic journey, during which you will travel to the lower world, to your soul garden, and to the Fire of Transformation in order to heal your toxic relationship patterns.

*[Short pause: 4 seconds]*

Make yourself comfortable, preferably lying down.

*[Short pause: 8 seconds]*

Start by focusing your attention on your breathing, and breathe deeply, in and out, in and out.

*[Short pause: 8 seconds]*

With each exhalation, you sink deeper and deeper into the surface on which you are lying.

*[Short pause: 8 seconds]*

Feel how you are being carried by Mother Earth.

*[Short pause: 8 seconds]*

Feel the air flowing through your nose and throat into your lungs.

*[Short pause: 8 seconds]*

Notice how your chest rises and falls in rhythm with your breath.

*[Short pause: 8 seconds]*

Focus all your attention on your breathing.

*[Short pause: 8 seconds]*

With each exhalation, let yourself sink deeper and deeper into the surface you are lying on, and release everything that is blocking and inhibiting you.

*[Short pause: 8 seconds]*

Images from your everyday life may drift into your mind. Don't hold onto them. Let them pass like clouds in the sky.

*[Short pause: 8 seconds]*

With every exhalation, sink deeper into the surface you are lying on.

*[Short pause: 8 seconds]*

Now, focus your attention completely on yourself. A flight of steps leading downwards appears in your mind's eye. A flight of seven steps.

*[Short pause: 8 seconds]*

You carefully move forward and descend step by step

*[Short pause: 4 seconds]*

. . . the first step

*[Short pause: 4 seconds]*

. . . the second step

*[Short pause: 4 seconds]*

. . . the third step

*[Short pause: 4 seconds]*

. . . the fourth step

*[Short pause: 4 seconds]*

. . . the fifth step

*[Short pause: 4 seconds]*

. . . the sixth step

*[Short pause: 4 seconds]*

. . . the seventh step.

*[Short pause: 4 seconds]*

When you reach the bottom, you see a gateway in front of you. This gateway is the entrance to the land of your soul, to your soul garden.

*[Short pause: 8 seconds]*

You walk slowly towards it and realize that the Guardian of this gate is already waiting for you.

*[Short pause: 8 seconds]*

First, notice what your Guardian looks like. Greet your Guardian, and ask them to lead you to the Fire of Transformation in your soul garden.

*[Short pause: 8 seconds]*

Together with your Guardian, you walk through the gateway and enter your soul garden: an infinitely wide and timeless landscape that reflects your fullness and beauty and your inner richness.

*[Short pause: 8 seconds]*

Your Guardian takes you on a path that leads you to the centre of your personal soul garden.

*[Short pause: 8 seconds]*

As you walk along this path, you gaze in wonder at your surroundings, your inner soul landscape.

*[Short pause: 8 seconds]*

The path leads to a place where a large fire with purple flames is burning. This is your inner Fire of Transformation.

*[Short pause: 8 seconds]*

Once there, sit down by the fire with your Guardian, and let the power, energy, and warmth of this place work its magic on you.

*[Short pause: 8 seconds]*

As you listen to the sound of the shamanic drum for five minutes, do what you came here to do to heal your toxic relationship patterns.

*[5 minutes drum]*

Thank the Fire of Transformation and all the beings involved for their help and support.

*[Short pause: 8 seconds]*

Now it is time to return home from your journey.

*[Short pause: 8 seconds]*

You say goodbye to the fire and the beings involved and go to the edge of the fireplace, where your Guardian is waiting for you.

*[Short pause: 8 seconds]*

Your Guardian leads you back to the entrance gateway of your soul garden.

*[Short pause: 8 seconds]*

As you walk along this path, you gaze again at your surroundings, your inner soul landscape.

*[Short pause: 8 seconds]*

When you arrive at the gateway, thank your Guardian for their guidance, say goodbye, and walk through the gateway.

*[Short pause: 8 seconds]*

In front of you, you see the flight of seven steps you descended at the beginning of your journey to your soul garden.

*[Short pause: 4 seconds]*

You walk towards it and slowly climb the seven steps.

*[Short pause: 4 seconds]*

. . . the seventh step

*[Short pause: 4 seconds]*

. . . the sixth step

*[Short pause: 4 seconds]*

. . . the fifth step

*[Short pause: 4 seconds]*

. . . the fourth step

*[Short pause: 4 seconds]*

. . . the third step

*[Short pause: 4 seconds]*

. . . the second step

*[Short pause: 4 seconds]*

. . . the first step.

*[Short pause: 4 seconds]*

Now you are back in the place within yourself where you started your journey.

*[Short pause: 8 seconds]*

Breathe deeply, in and out, and with each inhalation, slowly return to the here and now, to your everyday reality.

*[Short pause: 8 seconds]*

For a while, feel into what you have just experienced, and absorb it deeply.

*[Short pause: 8 seconds]*

Now open your eyes.

# RESOURCES

Information about the author's seminar and practice activities: **https://schamanenpfad.de**

Source of high-quality shamanic incense for the performance of incense rituals, for shamanic work, and for general accompaniment: **www.raeuchern-kreativ.de**

## Free Soul Journeys

You can find the following free downloads at **https://schamanenpfad.de**

○ The text for the "Journey into the Chamber of Self-Love" to reactivate your connection to self-love (see page 137)

○ A shamanic drumming sequence

## Online Courses

The following course is related to the themes covered in this book and can help you free yourself from toxic relationship patterns and heal your soul. More information on **https://schamanenpfad.de**.

○ Online training (English) – Integrative Shamanic Transformation Therapy

# Books

**Fromm, Erich.** *The Art of Loving*. London: HarperCollins Publishers/ Thorsons, 1995.

**Ingerman, Sandra.** *Soul Retrieval: Mending the Fragmented Self.* New York: HarperOne, revised and updated edition, 2006.

**Limmer, Stefan.** *Himmlisch lieben und göttlich vögeln: Rituale und Seelenreisen für Vertrauen und Hingabe.* Munich: Arkana, 2016.

_____*Die Macht der zwei Seelen in dir, Goldmann: Die Ahnen- und die Individualseele heilen und die eigene Bestimmung finden.* Munich: Goldmann Verlag, 2020. (Note: The Hero's Journey is described in detail in this book.)

_____*Rituale zum Loslassen: Wie wir ganz einfach Körper, Geist und Seele befreien.* Munich: Gräfe und Unzer Verlag, 2021.

_____*Versöhnung mit den Ahnen: Mit der 7-Generationen-Aufstellung zu ungeahnter Kraft* - Mit Übungs-CD. Munich: Arkana, 2015.

_____*Schamanische Seelenreisen* (mit CD): *Kraft und Heilung in sich selbst finden. Mit Übungen und Ritualen für den Alltag.* Munich: Gräfe und Unzer Verlag, 2014.

**Paturi, Felix, R.** *Heilbuch der Schamanen*. Regensburg: Reichel Verlag, 2008.

**Villoldo, Alberto.** *Shaman, Healer, Sage: How to Heal Yourself and Others with the Energy Medicine of the Americas.* New York: Harmony, 2000.

# RITUALS AND EXERCISES

# INDEX

# ABOUT THE AUTHOR

**Stefan Limmer** was born in 1964 in Regensburg, Germany. He is an initiated shaman, holistic practitioner, seminar leader, and biological building surveyor. In addition to naturopathic treatments, his practice focuses on shamanic healing methods, which he has been studying and applying for more than 20 years. This has resulted in a shamanic path that is optimally adapted to the needs, behavioural patterns, and clinical histories of Western people.

For Stefan Limmer, the key to healing toxic relationships lies in the shamanic approach to our soul. With the help of effective techniques, he has assisted hundreds of people on their path to a happy relationship.

For more information see: **https://schamanenpfad.de** and
**www.raeuchern-kreativ.de**